W9-AFU-618

Rick Steves®

SNAPSHOT

Northern Ireland

CONTENTS

INTRODUCTION

This Snapshot guide, excerpted from my guidebook *Rick Steves Ireland,* introduces you to Northern Ireland—an underrated and often overlooked part of the Emerald Isle that surprises visitors with its friendliness. I've included a lively mix of cities (Belfast and Derry), smaller towns (Portrush and Bangor), and plenty of lazy rural sights. History is palpable atop the brooding walls of Derry and in the remote and traditional countryside. And, while it's perfectly safe for a visit, Northern Ireland gives you a feel for Ireland's 20th-century "Troubles" as nowhere else—especially the provocative political murals in Derry's Bogside neighborhood, and on Belfast's Falls Road and Shankill Road. You'll also find enjoyable escapes: From the breezy seaside resort of Portrush, you can visit the scenic Antrim Coast—which boasts the unique staggered-columns geology of the Giant's Causeway, the spectacularly set Dunluce Castle, and a chance to sample whiskey at Old Bushmills Distillery.

To help you have the best trip possible, I've included the following topics in this book:

• **Planning Your Time,** with advice on how to make the most of your limited time

• **Orientation,** including tourist information (abbreviated as TI), tips on public transportation, local tour options, and helpful hints

• **Sights** with ratings:

▲▲▲—Don't miss

▲▲—Try hard to see

▲—Worthwhile if you can make it

No rating—Worth knowing about

• **Sleeping** and **Eating,** with good-value recommendations in every price range

  • **Connections,** with tips on trains, buses, and driving

Practicalities, near the end of this book, has information on money, staying connected, hotel reservations, transportation, and more.

To travel smartly, read this little book in its entirety before you go. It's my hope that this guide will make your trip more meaningful and rewarding. Traveling like a temporary local, you'll get the absolute most out of every mile, minute, and dollar.

Happy travels!

Rick Steves

NORTHERN IRELAND

NORTHERN IRELAND

Northern Ireland is a different country from the Republic—both politically (it's part of the United Kingdom) and culturally (a combination of Irish, Scottish, and English influences). Occupying the northern one-sixth of the island of Ireland, it's only about 13 miles from Scotland at the narrowest point of the North Channel, and bordered on the south and west by the Republic.

That border is almost invisible. But when you leave the Republic of Ireland and enter Northern Ireland, you *are* crossing an international border (although you don't have to flash your passport). The 2016 British referendum vote to leave the EU may change the way this border crossing is handled in the future, but for now it's business as usual (see "The Brexit Effect" sidebar, later).

You won't use euros here; Northern Ireland issues its own Ulster pound, which, like the Scottish pound, is interchangeable with the English pound (€1 = about £0.88; £1 = about $1.30). Price differences create a lively daily shopping trade for those living near the border. Some establishments near the border may take euros, but at a lousy exchange rate. Keep any euros for your return to the Republic, and get pounds from an ATM inside Northern Ireland instead. And if you're heading to Britain next, it's best to change your Ulster pounds into English ones (free at any bank in Northern Ireland, England, Wales, or Scotland).

A generation ago, Northern Ireland was a sadly contorted corner of the world. On my first visit, I remember thinking that even the name of this region sounded painful ("Ulster" seemed to me like a combination of "ulcer" and "blister"). But today, Northern Ireland has emerged from the dark shadow of the decades-long political strife and violence known as the Troubles. And while not as popular among tourists as its neighbor to the south, Northern Ireland offers plenty to see and do...and learn.

It's important for visitors to Northern Ireland to understand the ways in which its population is segregated along political, religious, and cultural lines. Roughly speaking, the eastern seaboard is more Unionist, Protestant, and of English-Scottish heritage, while the south and west (bordering the Republic of Ireland) are Nation-

Northern Ireland Almanac

Official Name: Since Northern Ireland (pronounced "Norn Iron" by locals) is not an independent state, there is no official country name. Some call it Ulster (although that has included three counties that today lie on the Republic's side of the border), while others label it the Six Counties.

Size: 5,400 square miles (about the size of Connecticut), constituting a sixth of the island. With 1.8 million people, it's the smallest of the four United Kingdom countries (the others are England, Wales, and Scotland).

Geography: Northern Ireland is shaped roughly like a doughnut, with the UK's largest lake in the middle (Lough Neagh, 150 square miles and a prime eel fishery). Gently rolling hills of green grass rise to the 2,800-foot Slieve Donard. The weather is temperate, cloudy, moist, windy, and hard to predict.

Latitude and Longitude: 54°N and 5°W (as far north as parts of the Alaskan panhandle).

Biggest Cities: Belfast, the capital, has 300,000 residents. Half a million people—nearly one in three Northern Irish—inhabit the greater Belfast area. Derry (called Londonderry by Unionists) has 95,000 people.

Economy: Northern Ireland's economy is more closely tied to the UK than to the Republic of Ireland, and is subsidized by the UK and EU. Traditional agriculture (potatoes and grain) is fading fast, though modern techniques and abundant grassland make Northern Ireland a major producer of sheep, cows, and grass seed. Modern software and communications companies are replacing traditional manufacturing. Shipyards are rusty relics, and the linen industry is now threadbare (both victims of cheaper labor in Asia).

Government: Northern Ireland is not a self-governing nation, but is part of the UK, ruled from London by Queen Elizabeth II and Prime Minister Theresa May, and represented by 18 elected Members of Parliament. For 50 years (1922-1972), Northern Ireland was granted a great deal of autonomy and self-governance, known as "Home Rule." The current National-

al Assembly (108-seat Parliament)—after an ineffective decade of political logjams—has recently begun to show signs of rejuvenation.

Flag: The official flag of Northern Ireland is the Union flag of the UK. But you'll also see the green, white, and orange Irish tricolor (waved by Nationalists) and the Northern Irish flag (white with a red cross and a red hand at its center), which is used by Unionists (see "The Red Hand of Ulster" sidebar on page 77).

alist, Catholic, and of indigenous Irish descent. Cities are often clearly divided between neighborhoods of one group or the other. Early in life, locals learn to identify the highly symbolic (and highly charged) colors, jewelry, music, names, accents, and vocabulary that distinguish the cultural groups.

Over the last century, the conflict between these two groups has been not about faith, but about politics: Will Northern Ireland stay part of the United Kingdom (Unionists), or become part of the Republic of Ireland (Nationalists)?

The roots of Protestant and Catholic differences date back to the time when Ireland was a colony of Great Britain. Four hundred years ago, Protestant settlers from England and Scotland were strategically "planted" in Catholic Ireland to help assimilate the island into the British economy. In 1620, the dominant English powerbase in London felt entitled to call both islands—Ireland as well as Britain—the "British Isles" on maps (a geographic label that irritates Irish Nationalists to this day). These Protestant settlers established their own cultural toehold on the island, laying claim to the most fertile land. Might made right, and God was on their side. Meanwhile, the underdog Catholic Irish held strong to their Gaelic culture on their ever-diminishing, boggy, rocky farms.

By the beginning of the 20th century, the sparse Protestant population could no longer control the entire island. When Ireland won its independence in 1921 (after a bloody guerrilla war against British rule), 26 of the island's 32 counties became the Irish Free State, ruled from Dublin with dominion status in the British Commonwealth—similar to Canada's level of sovereignty. In 1949, these 26 counties left the Commonwealth altogether and became the Republic of Ireland, severing all political ties with Britain. Meanwhile, the six remaining northeastern counties—the only ones with a Protestant majority who considered themselves British—chose not to join the Irish Free State and remained part of the UK.

But within these six counties—now joined as the political entity called Northern Ireland—was a large, disaffected Irish (mostly Catholic) minority who felt marginalized by the drawing of the new international border. This sentiment was represented by the Irish Republican Army (IRA), who wanted all 32 of Ireland's counties to be united in one Irish nation—their political goals were "Nationalist." Their political opponents were the "Unionists"—Protestant British eager to defend the union with Britain, who were primarily led by two groups: the long-established Orange Order, and the military muscle of the newly mobilized Ulster Volunteer Force (UVF).

In World War II, the Republic stayed neutral while the North enthusiastically supported the Allied cause—winning a spot close

to London's heart. Derry (a.k.a. Londonderry) became an essential Allied convoy port, while Belfast lost more than 800 civilians during four Luftwaffe bombing raids in 1941. After the war, the split between North and South seemed permanent, and Britain invested heavily in Northern Ireland to bring it solidly into the UK fold.

In the Republic of Ireland (the South), where the population was 94 percent Catholic and only 6 percent Protestant, there was a clearly dominant majority. But in the North, at the time it was formed, Catholics were a sizable 35 percent of the population—enough to demand attention when they complained about anti-Catholic discrimination on the part of the Protestant government. It was this discrimination that led to the Troubles, the conflict that filled headlines from the late 1960s to the late 1990s.

Partly inspired by Martin Luther King Jr. and the civil rights movement in America—beamed into Irish living rooms by the new magic of television news—in the 1960s the Catholic minority in Northern Ireland began a nonviolent struggle to end discrimination, advocating for better jobs and housing. Extremists polarized issues, and once-peaceful demonstrations—also broadcast on TV news—became violent.

Unionists were afraid that if the island became one nation, the relatively poor Republic of Ireland would drag down the compara-tively affluent North, and feared losing political power to a Catholic majority. As the two sides clashed in 1969, the British Army entered the fray. Their role, initially a peacekeeping one, gradually evolved into acting as muscle for the Unionist government. In 1972, a tragic watershed year, more than 500 people died as combatants moved from petrol bombs to guns, and a new, more violent IRA emerged. In the 30-year (1968-1998) chapter of the struggle for an indepen-dent and united Ireland, more than 3,000 people died.

In the 1990s—with the UK (and Ireland's) membership in the EU, the growth of its economy, and the weakening of the Catho-lic Church's authority—the influence of the Republic of Ireland became less threatening to the Unionists. Optimists hailed the signing of a breakthrough peace plan in 1998, called the "Good Friday Peace Accord" by Nationalists, or the "Belfast Agreement" by Unionists. This led to the release of political prisoners on both sides in 2000—a highly emotional event.

British Army surveillance towers in Northern Ireland cit-ies were dismantled in 2006, and the army formally ended its 38-year-long Operation Banner campaign in 2007. In 2010, the peace process was jolted forward by a surprisingly forthright apol-ogy offered by then British Prime Minister David Cameron, who expressed regret for the British Army's offenses on Bloody Sun-day. The apology was prompted by the Saville Report—the results of an investigation conducted by the UK government as part of the Good Friday Peace Accord. It found that the 1972 shootings of Nationalist civil-rights marchers on Bloody Sunday by British soldiers was "unjustified" and the victims innocent (vindication for the victims' families, who had fought since 1972 to clear their loved ones' names).

Major hurdles to a lasting peace persist, but downtown check-points and "bomb-damage clearance sales" have been gone for de-cades. Replacing them are a forest of construction cranes, especial-ly in rejuvenated Belfast. Tourists in Northern Ireland were once considered courageous (or reckless). Today, more tourists than ever are venturing north to Belfast and Derry, and cruise-ship crowds disembark in Belfast to board charter buses that fan out to visit the Giant's Causeway and Old Bushmills Distillery.

When locals spot you with a map and a lost look on your face, they're likely to ask, "Wot yer lookin fer?" in their distinc-tive Northern accent. They're not suspicious of you, but trying to help you find your way. They may even "giggle" (Google) it for you. You're safer in Belfast than in many UK cities—and far safer, statistically, than in most major US cities. You'd have to look for trouble to find it here. Just don't seek out spit-and-sawdust pubs in working-class neighborhoods and spew simplistic opinions about

Northern Ireland Terminology

You may hear Northern Ireland referred to as **Ulster**—the traditional name of Ireland's ancient northernmost province. When the Republic of Ireland became independent in 1922, six of the nine counties of Ulster elected to form Northern Ireland, while three counties joined the Republic.

The mostly Protestant **Unionist** majority—and the more hardline, working-class **Loyalists**—want the North to remain in the UK. The **Ulster Unionist Party** (UUP) is the political party representing moderate Unionist views (Nobel Peace Prize co-winner David Trimble led the UUP from 1995 to 2005). The **Democratic Unionist Party** (DUP) takes a harder stance in defense of Unionism. The **Ulster Volunteer Force** (UVF), the **Ulster Freedom Fighters** (UFF), and the **Ulster Defense Association** (UDA) are Loyalist paramilitary organizations: All three are labeled "proscribed groups" by the UK's 2000 Terrorism Act.

The mostly Catholic **Nationalist** minority—and the more hardline, working-class **Republicans**—want a united and independent Ireland ruled by Dublin. The **Social Democratic Labor Party** (SDLP), founded by Nobel Peace Prize co-winner John Hume, is the moderate political party representing Nationalist views. **Sinn Fein** takes a harder stance in defense of Nationalism. The **Irish Republican Army** (IRA) is the now-disarmed Nationalist paramilitary organization formerly linked with Sinn Fein. The **Alliance Party** wants to bridge the gap between Unionists and Nationalists.

The long-simmering struggle to settle Northern Ireland's national identity precipitated the **Troubles,** the violent, 30-year conflict (1968-1998) between Unionist and Nationalist factions. To gain more insight into the complexity of the Troubles, the 90-minute documentary *Voices from the Grave* provides an excellent overview (easy to find on YouTube). Also check out the University of Ulster's informative and evenhanded Conflict Archive at http://cain.ulst.ac.uk/index.html.

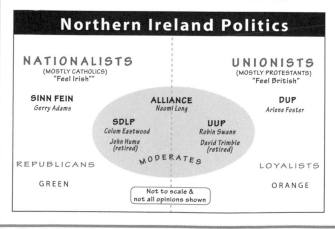

Northern Ireland Politics

NATIONALISTS
(MOSTLY CATHOLICS)
"Feel Irish"

UNIONISTS
(MOSTLY PROTESTANTS)
"Feel British"

SINN FEIN
Gerry Adams

ALLIANCE
Naomi Long

DUP
Arlene Foster

SDLP
Colum Eastwood

UUP
Robin Swann

John Hume
(retired)

David Trimble
(retired)

MODERATES

REPUBLICANS

LOYALISTS

GREEN

ORANGE

Not to scale &
not all opinions shown

The Brexit Effect

A hundred years ago, the British Isles were ruled from one place: London. Today, three sections of this geographic area (Ireland, Scotland, and England/Wales) drift in separate directions. And Northern Ireland, with strong cultural, geographic, and economic connections to all three, is being stretched uncomfortably.

In 2016, the people of the United Kingdom narrowly approved a referendum to leave the European Union (the "Brexit"). But in Northern Ireland (as in Scotland), a majority of people voted to stay. So where does that leave their relationship with the English and Welsh, who predominately voted to exit?

Among the Unionist community in the North, most of their ancestors came across from Scotland, with cherished cultural ties still evident. But Scotland is flirting with staying in the EU (and separating from the UK). The Republic of Ireland fills 80 percent of the island of Ireland, and a large minority in the North would like to see the island as a single Irish nation. Which direction will the North lean? Special status within the UK? Reunification with the Republic?

When the UK leaves the EU, the current "soft border" between the Republic and Northern Ireland will be reevaluated. It's not yet clear what form the new border will take. Few want the hassle and economic complications of a "hard border" (trade tariffs and border controls between EU and non-EU zones). People over 30 also remember the days when the border between Northern Ireland and the Republic was a closely patrolled line in a war zone. A hard border could rekindle tension between dormant Republican and Loyalist extremists. Borders add fuel to "them and us" perceptions.

Stay tuned to see how the swirling currents of Brexit, the Scottish independence movement, and the Irish reunification dream will affect this unique corner of the world...perched precariously between diverging cultural and economic powers: Ireland, Scotland, and England.

sensitive local topics. Tourists notice lingering tension mainly during the "marching season" (Easter-Aug, peaking in early July). July 12—"the Twelfth"—is traditionally the most confrontational day of the year in the North, when proud Protestant Unionist Orangemen march to celebrate their Britishness (often through staunchly Nationalist Catholic neighborhoods—it's still good advice to lie low if you stumble onto any big Orange parades).

As the less-fractured Northern Ireland enters the 21st century, one of its most valuable assets is its industrious people—and their legendary work ethic. When they emigrated to the US, they became known as the Scots-Irish and played a crucial role in our nation's founding. They were signers of our Declaration of Independence, a dozen of our presidents, and the ancestors of Davy Crockett and Mark Twain.

Northern Irish workers have a proclivity for making things that go. They've produced far-reaching inventions like Dunlop's first inflatable tire. The Shorts aircraft factory (in Belfast) built the Wright Brothers' first six aircraft for commercial sale and the world's first vertical takeoff jet. The *Titanic* was the only flop of Northern Ireland's otherwise successful shipbuilding industry. The once-futuristic DeLorean sports car was made in Belfast.

Notable people from Northern Ireland include musicians Van Morrison and James Galway, and actors Liam Neeson, Roma Downey, Ciarán Hinds, and Kenneth Branagh. The North also produced Christian intellectual and writer C. S. Lewis, Victorian physicist Lord Kelvin, engineer Harry Ferguson (inventor of the modern farm tractor and first four-wheel drive Formula One car), and soccer-star playboy George Best—who once famously remarked, "I spent most of my money on liquor and women...and the rest I wasted."

As in the Republic, sports are big in the North. Northern-born golfers Rory McIlroy, Graeme McDowell, and Darren Clarke have won a fistful of majors over the past decade, filling local hearts with pride. With close ties to Scotland, many Northern Irish fans follow the exploits of Glasgow soccer teams—but which team you root for betrays which side of the tracks you come from. Those who cheer for Glasgow Celtic are Nationalist and Catholic; those waving banners for the Glasgow Rangers are Unionist and Protestant. To maintain peace, some pubs post signs on their doors banning patrons from wearing sports jerseys. Luckily, sports with no sectarian history are now being introduced, such as the Belfast Giants ice hockey team— a hit with both communities.

Northern Ireland seems poised to do great things. As you travel through Northern Ireland today, you'll encounter a fascinating country with a complicated, often tragic history—and a brightening future.

DERRY

No city in Ireland connects the kaleidoscope of historical dots more colorfully than Derry. From a leafy monastic hamlet to a Viking-pillaged port, from a cannonball-battered siege survivor to an Industrial Revolution sweatshop, from an essential WWII naval base to a wrenching flashpoint of sectarian Troubles... Derry has seen it all.

Though Belfast is the capital of Northern Ireland, this pivotal city has a more diverse history and a prettier setting. Derry was a vibrant city back when Belfast was just a mudflat. With roughly a third of Belfast's population (95,000), Derry feels more welcoming and manageable to visitors.

The town is the mecca of Ulster Unionism. When Ireland was being divvied up, the River Foyle was the logical border between the North and the Republic. But, for sentimental and economic reasons, the North kept Derry, which is otherwise on the Republic's side of the river. Consequently, this predominantly Catholic-Nationalist city was much contested throughout the Troubles.

Even its name is disputed. While most of its population and its city council call it "Derry," some maps, road signs, and all UK train schedules use "Londonderry," the name on its 1662 royal charter and the one favored by Unionists. I once asked a Northern Ireland rail employee for a ticket to "Derry"; he replied that there was no such place, but he would sell me one to "Londonderry." I'll call it Derry in this book since that's what the majority of the city's inhabitants do.

The past 15 years have brought some refreshing changes. Manned British Army surveillance towers were taken down in 2006, and most British troops finally departed in mid-2007, after

38 years in Northern Ireland. In June 2011, a new, curvy pedestrian bridge across the River Foyle was completed. Locals dubbed it the Peace Bridge because it links the predominantly Protestant Waterside (east bank) with the predominantly Catholic Cityside (west bank). Today, you can feel comfortable wandering the streets and enjoying this "legend-Derry" city.

PLANNING YOUR TIME

If just passing through (say, on your way to Portrush), it takes a few hours to see the essential Derry sights: Visit the Tower Museum and catch some views from the town wall.

With more time, spend a night in Derry, so you can see the powerful Bogside murals and take a walking tour around the town walls—you'll appreciate this underrated city. With two nights in Derry, consider crossing back into the Republic for a scenic driving loop through part of remote County Donegal.

Orientation to Derry

The River Foyle flows north, slicing Derry into eastern and western chunks. The old town walls and almost all worthwhile sights are on the west side. (The tiny train station and Ebrington Square—at the end of the Peace Bridge—are the main reasons to spend time on the east side.) Waterloo Place and the adjacent Guildhall Square, just outside the north corner of the old city walls, are the pedestrian hubs of city activity. The Strand Road area extending north from Waterloo Place makes a comfortable home base, with the majority of lodging and restaurant suggestions within a block or two. The Diamond (main square) and its War Memorial statue mark the heart of the old city within the walls.

TOURIST INFORMATION

The TI sits on the riverfront and rents bikes (£5/2 hours, £8/4 hours, £12/8 hours), and can book bus and walking tours (Mon-Sat 9:00-18:00, Sun 10:00-17:00, closes earlier in off-season; 44 Foyle Street, tel. 028/7126-7284, www.visitderry.com).

ARRIVAL IN DERRY

By Train: Next to the river on the east side of town, Derry's little end-of-the-line train station (no storage lockers) has service to Portrush, Belfast, and Dublin. Each arriving train is greeted by free shuttle buses to Ulsterbus Station on the west side of town, a couple of minutes' walk south of Guildhall Square on Foyle Street (luggage storage at post office around corner in same building, fee based on bag size, Mon-Fri 9:30-17:30—beware of lunch closure, closed Sat-Sun). Otherwise, it's a £5 taxi ride to Guildhall Square.

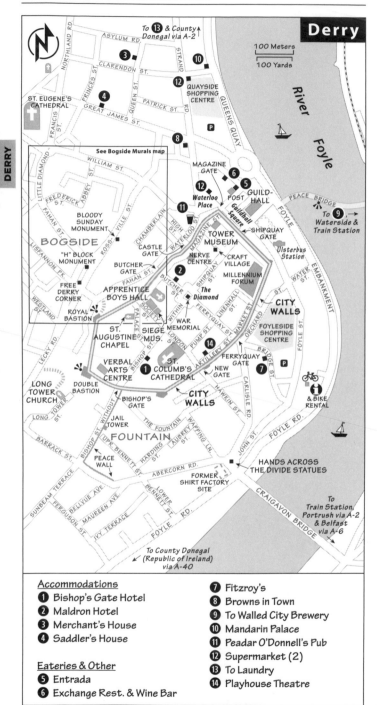

DERRY

Derry

100 Meters
100 Yards

River Foyle

To ⑬ & County Donegal via A-2

ST. EUGENE'S CATHEDRAL

NORTHLAND RD.
ASYLUM RD.
CLARENDON ST.
PRINCES ST.
GREAT JAMES ST.
FRANCIS ST.
QUEEN ST.
PATRICK ST.
STRAND RD.
QUEENS QUAY

③
④
⑩
⑫ QUAYSIDE SHOPPING CENTRE
⑧

See Bogside Murals map

LITTLE DIAMOND
WILLIAM ST.
FREDERICK ST.
FAHAN ST.
ABBEY ST.
ROSS-VILLE ST.
CHAMBERLAIN ST.
LISFANNON PK.
WESTLAND ST.
LECKY RD.

BOGSIDE

BLOODY SUNDAY MONUMENT
"H" BLOCK MONUMENT
BUTCHER GATE
FREE DERRY CORNER
APPRENTICE BOYS HALL
ROYAL BASTION
SIEGE MUS.
ST. AUGUSTINE CHAPEL
VERBAL ARTS CENTRE
LONG TOWER CHURCH
DOUBLE BASTION
BISHOP'S GATE
JAIL TOWER

CASTLE GATE
NERVE CENTRE
②
THE DIAMOND
WAR MEMORIAL
① ST. COLUMB'S CATHEDRAL
NEW GATE
⑭
PUMP ST.
FERRYQUAY ST.
LINENHALL ST.
MARKET ST.
ARTILLERY ST.
HAWKIN ST.

MAGAZINE GATE
⑫ WATERLOO PLACE
⑪
⑥
⑤ POST
GUILD-HALL
Guildhall Square
TOWER MUSEUM
CRAFT VILLAGE
MILLENNIUM FORUM
SHIPQUAY GATE
Ulsterbus Station
FOYLE
PEACE BRIDGE
To ⑨ Waterside & Train Station
WATER ST.
EMBANKMENT
CITY WALLS
FOYLESIDE SHOPPING CENTRE
FERRYQUAY GATE
⑦
ORCHARD ST.
BRIDGE ST.
FOYLE ST.

CITY WALLS

FOUNTAIN
PEACE WALL
BARRACK ST.
SUNBEAM TERRACE
FERGUSON AVE.
BELLVUE AVE.
MAUREEN AVE.
IVY TERRACE
LOWER BENNETT ST.
UPR. BENNETT ST.
HARDING ST.
AUBREY ST.
WAPPING LN.
THE FOUNTAIN
ABERCORN RD.
FORMER SHIRT FACTORY SITE
FOYLE RD.
CARLISLE RD.
JOHN ST.

HANDS ACROSS THE DIVIDE STATUES

& BIKE RENTAL

CRAIGAVON BRIDGE

To Train Station, Portrush via A-2 & Belfast via A-6

To County Donegal (Republic of Ireland) via A-40

Accommodations
❶ Bishop's Gate Hotel
❷ Maldron Hotel
❸ Merchant's House
❹ Saddler's House

Eateries & Other
❺ Entrada
❻ Exchange Rest. & Wine Bar

❼ Fitzroy's
❽ Browns in Town
❾ To Walled City Brewery
❿ Mandarin Palace
⓫ Peadar O'Donnell's Pub
⓬ Supermarket (2)
⓭ To Laundry
⓮ Playhouse Theatre

The same free shuttle service leaves Ulsterbus Station 15 minutes before each departing train. Unfortunately, there's not yet a footpath from the train station to the pedestrian Peace Bridge.

By Bus: All intercity buses stop at the Ulsterbus Station, on Foyle Street close to Guildhall Square.

By Car: Drivers stopping for a few hours can park at the Foyleside parking garage across from the TI (£1/hour, £3/4 hours, Mon-Sat 8:00-19:00 or later, Sun from 12:00, tel. 028/7137-7575). Drivers staying overnight can ask about parking at their B&B, or try the Quayside parking garage behind the Travelodge (£0.80/hour, £3/4 hours, £8 additional for overnight, daily 7:30-21:00, closes earlier on weekends).

HELPFUL HINTS

Money: Danske Bank is on Guildhall Square and the Bank of Ireland is on Strand Road.

Bookstore: Foyle Books is a dusty little pleasure for random browsing (Mon-Sat 11:00-17:00, closed Sun, 12 Magazine Street at entrance to Craft Village, tel. 028/7137-2530).

Laundry: Bubbles has drop-off service—bring it in the morning, pick up later that day (Mon-Fri 9:00-17:00, Sat from 10:00, closed Sun, 141 Strand Road, tel. 028/7136-3366).

Taxi: Try **City Cabs** (tel. 028/7126-4466), **The Taxi Company** (tel. 028/7126-2626), or **Foyle Taxis** (tel. 028/7127-9999).

Car Rental: Enterprise is handy (70 Clooney Road, tel. 028/7186-1699, www.enterprise.co.uk). Another option is **Desmond Motors** (173 Strand Road, tel. 028/7136-7136, www. desmondmotors.co.uk).

Tours in Derry

Walking Tours

McCrossan's City Tours leads insightful hour-long walks, giving a rounded view of the city's history. Tours depart from 11 Carlisle Road, just below Ferryquay Gate (£4; daily at 10:00, 12:00, 14:00, and 16:00; tel. 028/7127-1996, mobile 077-1293-7997, www. derrycitytours.com, derrycitytours@aol.com). They also offer private tours (one-hour city tour-£25).

Bogside History Tours offers walks led by Bogside residents who lost loved ones in the tragic events of Bloody Sunday (£6, £9 combo-ticket with Museum of Free Derry; April-Sept daily at 11:00 and 13:00, Mon-Fri also at 15:00; depart from in front of the Guildhall, mobile 077-3145-0088 or 078-0056-7165, www. bogside-history-tours.com, paul@bogsidehistorytours.com). Tour guides also offer various taxi tours (£25/hour, call or email for options).

Hop-On, Hop-Off Bus Tour

City Sightseeing's double-decker buses are a good option for a general overview of Derry. The one-hour loop covers both sides of the river (seven stops overall), including the Guildhall, the old city walls, political wall murals, cathedrals, and former shirt factories. Your ticket is good for 24 hours (£12.50, pay driver, bus departs April-Sept daily on the hour 10:00-16:00 from in front of TI and Guildhall Square, tel. 028/7137-0067, www.citysightseeingderry.com).

City Sightseeing also offers trips from Derry to the Giant's Causeway, Dunluce Castle, Old Bushmills Distillery, and Carrick-a-Rede Rope Bridge in County Antrim (£25, price does not include Bushmills entry, runs daily May-Sept, depart TI at 10:00, return by 17:00, minimum 10 people). In addition, they offer tours to Glenveagh National Park in County Donegal (depart TI at 9:00, return by 15:00, minimum 10 people). You can book any of their tours online or by phone.

Walks in Derry

Though calm today, Derry is stamped by years of tumultuous conflict. These two self-guided walks (each taking less than an hour) will increase your understanding of the town's history. Walk the Walls, starting on the old city walls and ending at the Anglican Cathedral, focuses on Derry's early days. My Bogside Murals Walk guides you to the city's compelling murals, which document the time of the Troubles. These tours, each worth ▲▲, can be done separately or linked, depending on your time.

WALK THE WALLS

Squatting determinedly in the city center, the old city walls of Derry (built 1613-1618 and still intact, except for wider gates to handle modern vehicles) hold an almost mythic place in Irish history.

It was here in 1688 that a group of brave apprentice boys, some of whom had been shipped to Derry as orphans after the great fire of London in 1666, made their stand. They slammed the city gates shut in the face of the approaching Catholic forces of deposed King James II. With this act, the boys gal-vanized the city's indecisive Protes-tant defenders inside the walls.

Months of negotiations and a grinding 105-day siege followed, during which a third of the 20,000 refugees and defenders crammed into the city perished. The siege was finally broken in 1689, when supply ships broke through a boom stretched across the River Foyle. The sacrifice and defiant survival of the city turned the tide in favor of newly crowned Protestant King William of Orange, who arrived in Ireland soon after and defeated James at the pivotal Battle of the Boyne.

To fully appreciate the walls, take a walk on top of them (free and open from dawn to dusk). Almost 20 feet high and at least as thick, the walls form a mile-long oval loop that you can cover in less than an hour. But the most interesting section is the half-circuit facing the Bogside, starting at Magazine Gate (stairs face the Tower Museum Derry inside the walls) and finishing at Bishop's Gate.

• *Enter the walls at Magazine Gate and find the stairs opposite the Tower Museum. Once atop the walls, head left.*

Walk the wall as it heads uphill, snaking along the earth's contours. In the row of buildings on the left (just before crossing over Castle Gate), you'll see an arch entry into the **Craft Village,** an alley lined with a cluster of cute shops and cafés that showcase the economic rejuvenation of Derry (Mon-Sat 9:30-17:30, closed Sun).

• *After crossing over Butcher Gate, stop in front of the grand building with the four columns to view the...*

First Derry Presbyterian Church: This impressive-looking building is the second church to occupy this site. The first was built by Queen Mary in the 1690s to thank the Presbyterian community for standing by their Anglican brethren during the dark days of the famous siege. That church was later torn down to make room for today's stately Neoclassical, red-sandstone church finished in 1780. Over the next 200 years, time took its toll on the structure, which was eventually closed due to dry rot and Republican firebombings. But in 2011, the renovated church reopened to a chorus of cross-community approval (yet one more sign of the slow reconciliation taking place in Derry). The **Blue Coat School** exhibit behind the church highlights the important role of Presbyterians in local history (free but donation encouraged, closed Sat-Tue in summer and all of Oct-April, tel. 028/7126-1550).

• *Just up the block is the...*

Apprentice Boys Memorial Hall: Built in 1873, this houses the private lodge and meeting rooms of an all-male Protestant organization. The group is dedicated to the memory of the original 13 apprentice boys who saved the day during the 1688 siege. Each year, on the Saturday closest to the August 12 anniversary date, the modern-day Apprentice Boys Society celebrates the end of the siege with a controversial march atop the walls. These walls are considered sacred ground for devout Unionists, who claim that many who died during the famous siege were buried within

DERRY

Derry's History

Once an island in the River Foyle, Derry (from *doire,* Irish for "oak grove") was chosen by St. Colmcille (St. Columba in English) circa A.D. 546 for a monastic settlement. He later banished himself to the island of Iona in Scotland out of remorse for sparking a bloody battle over the rights to a holy manuscript that he had secretly copied.

A thousand years later, the English defeated the last Ulster-based Gaelic chieftains in the Battle of Kinsale (1601). With victory at hand, the English took advantage of the power vacuum. They began the "plantation" of Ulster with loyal Protestant subjects imported from Scotland and England. The native Irish were displaced to less desirable rocky or boggy lands, sowing the seeds of resentment that eventually fueled the Troubles.

A dozen wealthy London guilds (grocers, haberdashers, tailors, and others) took on Derry as an investment and changed its name to "Londonderry." They built the last great walled city in Ireland to protect their investment from the surrounding—and hostile—Irish locals. The walls proved their worth in 1688-1689, when the town's Protestant defenders, loyal to King William of Orange, withstood a prolonged siege by the forces of Catholic King James II. "No surrender" is still a passionate rallying cry among Ulster Unionists determined to remain part of the United Kingdom.

The town became a major port of emigration to the New World in the early 1800s. Then, when the Industrial Revolution provided a steam-powered sewing factory, the city developed a thriving shirt-making industry. The factories here employed mostly Catholic women who had honed their skills in rural County Donegal. Although Belfast grew larger and wealthier, Unionists tightened their grip on "Londonderry" and the walls that they regarded with almost holy reverence. In 1921, they insisted that the city be included in Northern Ireland when the province was partitioned from the new Irish Free State (later to become the Republic of Ireland). A bit of gerrymandering (with three lightly populated Unionist districts outvoting two densely populated

the battered walls because of lack of space. The **Siege Museum** stands behind the hall, giving a narrow-focus Unionist view of the siege (£3, Mon-Sat 10:00-16:30, closed Sun, 18 Society Street, tel. 028/7126-1219).

Next, you'll pass a large, square pedestal on the right atop Royal Bastion. It once supported a column in honor of Governor

Nationalist districts) ensured that the Protestant minority maintained control of the city, despite its Catholic majority.

Derry was a key escort base for US convoys headed for Britain during World War II, and 60 surviving German U-boats were instructed to surrender here at the end of the war. After the war, poor Catholics—unable to find housing—took over the abandoned military barracks, with multiple families living in each dwelling. Only homeowners were allowed to vote, and the Unionist minority, which controlled city government, was not eager to build more housing that would tip the voting balance away from them. Over the years, sectarian pressures gradually built—until they reached the boiling point. The ugly events of Bloody Sunday on January 30, 1972, brought worldwide attention to the Troubles (for more details, see "Bloody Sunday" sidebar on page 23).

Today, life has stabilized in Derry, and the population has increased by 25 percent in the last 30 years. The Foyleside Shopping Centre, bankrolled by investors from Boston, opened in 1995. The 1998 Good Friday Peace Accord provided significant progress toward peace, and the British Army withdrew 90 percent of its troops in mid-2007. With a population that is over 70 percent Catholic, the city has agreed to alternate Nationalist and Unionist mayors. There is a feeling of cautious optimism as Derry—the epicenter of bombs and bloody conflicts in the 1960s and 1970s—now boasts a history museum that airs all viewpoints.

The city continues to work on building a happier image. The wall—with all its troubled imagery and once nicknamed "the noose"—is now called "the necklace." With its complicated history, you're damned-if-you-do and damned-if-you-don't when it comes to calling it Derry (pro-Catholic, Nationalist) or Londonderry (pro-Protestant, Unionist). Some call it Derry/Londonderry or Londonderry/Derry. Others just say "Slashtown." And the tourist board calls it "legend-Derry."

George Walker, the commander of the defenders during the famous siege. In 1972, the IRA blew up the column, which had 105 steps to the top (one for each day of the siege). An adjacent plaque shows a photo of the column before it was destroyed.

• *Opposite the empty pedestal is the small Anglican...*

St. Augustine Chapel: Set in a pretty graveyard, this Anglican chapel is where some believe the original sixth-century monastery of St. Columba stood. The quaint grounds are open to visitors (Mon-Sat 10:30-16:30, closed Sun except for worship). In Victorian times, this stretch of the walls was a fashionable promenade walk.

As you walk, you'll pass a long wall (on the left)—all that's left of a former **British Army base,** which stood here until 2006. Two 50-foot towers used to loom out of it, bristling with cameras and listening devices. Soldiers built them here for a bird's-eye view of the once-turbulent Catholic Bogside district below. The towers' dismantlement—as well as the removal of most of the British Army from Northern Ireland—is another positive sign in cautiously optimistic Derry. The walls of this former army base now contain a parking lot.

Stop at the **Double Bastion** fortified platform that occupies this corner of the city walls. The old cannon is nicknamed "Roaring Meg" for the fury of its firing during the siege.

From here, you can see across the Bogside to the not-so-faraway hills of County Donegal in the Republic. Derry was once an island, but as the River Foyle gradually changed its course, the area you see below the wall began to drain. Over time, and especially after the Great Potato Famine (1845-1849), Catholic peasants from rural Donegal began to move into Derry to find work during the Industrial Revolution. They settled on this least desirable land...on the soggy bog side of the city. From this vantage point, survey the Bogside with its political murals and Palestinian flags.

Directly below and to the right are Free Derry Corner and Rossville Street, where the tragic events of Bloody Sunday took place in 1972. Down on the left is the 18th-century Long Tower Catholic church, named after the monk-built round tower that once stood in the area.

• *Head to the grand brick building behind you. This is the...*

Verbal Arts Centre: A former Presbyterian school, this center promotes the development of local literary arts in the form of poetry, drama, writing, and storytelling. You can drop in and see what performances might be on during your visit (Mon-Fri 9:00-17:00, Sat 12:00-14:00, closed Sun, tel. 028/7126-6946, www.verbalartscentre.co.uk).

• *Go left another 50 yards around the corner to reach...*

Bishop's Gate: From here, look up Bishop Street Within (inside the walls). This was the site of another British Army surveillance tower. Placed just inside the town walls, it overlooked the neighborhood until 2006. Now look in the other direction to see Bishop Street Without (outside the walls). You'll spot a modern wall topped by a high mesh fence, running along the left side of Bishop Street Without.

This is a so-called **"peace wall,"** built to ensure the security of the Protestant enclave living behind it in Derry's Fountain neighborhood. When the Troubles reignited almost 50 years ago, 20,000 Protestants lived on this side of the river. This small housing development of 1,000 people is all that remains of that proud community today. The rest have chosen to move across the river to the mostly Protestant Waterside district. The stone tower halfway down the "peace wall" is all that remains of the old jail that briefly held doomed rebels after a 1798 revolt against the British.

• *From Bishop's Gate, those short on time can descend from the walls and walk 15 minutes directly back through the heart of the old city, along Bishop Street Within and Shipquay Street to Guildhall Square. With more time, consider visiting St. Columb's Cathedral, the Long Tower Church, and the murals of the Bogside.*

BOGSIDE MURALS WALK

The Catholic Bogside area was the tinderbox of the modern Troubles in Northern Ireland. Bloody Sunday, a terrible confrontation during a march that occurred nearly 50 years ago, sparked a sectarian inferno, and the ashes have not yet fully cooled. Today, the murals of the Bogside give visitors an accessible glimpse of this community's passionate perception of those events.

Getting There: The events are memorialized in 12 murals painted on the ends of residential flats along a 300-yard stretch of Rossville Street and Lecky Road, where the march took place. For the purposes of this walk, you can reach them from Waterloo Place via William Street. They are also accessible from the old city walls at Butcher Gate via the long set of stairs extending below Fahan Street on the grassy hillside, or by the stairs leading down from the Long Tower Church. These days, this neighborhood is gritty but quiet and safe.

The Artists: Two brothers, Tom and William Kelly, and their childhood friend Kevin Hasson are known as the Bogside Artists. They grew up in the Bogside and witnessed the tragic events that took place there, which led them to begin painting the murals in 1994. One of the brothers, Tom, gained a reputation as a "heritage mural" painter, specializing in scenes of life in the old days. In a surprising and hopeful development, Tom was later invited into Derry's Protestant Fountain neighborhood to work with a youth club there on three proud heritage murals that were painted over paramilitary graffiti. For more about this unique trio, visit their website, BogsideArtists.com.

DERRY

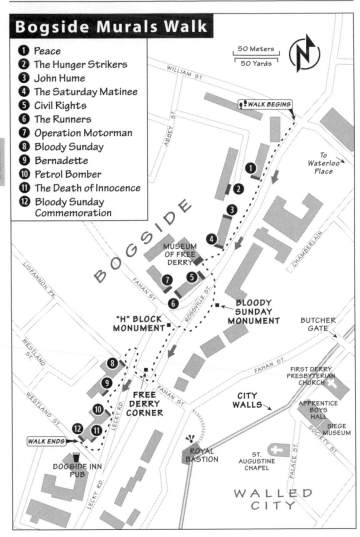

Bogside Murals Walk

1 Peace
2 The Hunger Strikers
3 John Hume
4 The Saturday Matinee
5 Civil Rights
6 The Runners
7 Operation Motorman
8 Bloody Sunday
9 Bernadette
10 Petrol Bomber
11 The Death of Innocence
12 Bloody Sunday
   Commemoration

50 Meters
50 Yards

WILLIAM ST.

WALK BEGINS

To Waterloo Place

ABBEY ST.

CHAMBERLAIN

B O G S I D E

MUSEUM OF FREE DERRY

LISFANNON PK.

FAHAN ST.

ROSSVILLE ST.

BLOODY SUNDAY MONUMENT

BUTCHER GATE

"H" BLOCK MONUMENT

WESTLAND ST.

FAHAN ST.

FIRST DERRY PRESBYTERIAN CHURCH

WESTLAND ST.

LECKY RD.

FREE DERRY CORNER

FAHAN ST.

CITY WALLS

APPRENTICE BOYS HALL

SIEGE MUSEUM

SOCIETY ST.

WALK ENDS

BOGSIDE INN PUB

LECKY RD.

ROYAL BASTION

ST. AUGUSTINE CHAPEL

PALACE ST.

W A L L E D C I T Y

The Murals: Start out at the corner of Rossville and William streets.

The Bogside murals face different directions (and some are partially hidden by buildings), so they're not all visible from a single viewpoint. Plan on walking three long blocks along Rossville Street (which becomes Lecky Road) to see them all. Residents are used to visitors and don't mind if you photograph the murals. Local motorists are uncommonly courteous with allowing visitors to cross the busy street.

From William Street, walk south along the right side of Ross-

Bloody Sunday

Inspired by civil rights marches in America in the mid-1960s, and the Prague Spring uprising and Paris student strikes of 1968, civil rights groups began to protest in Northern Ireland around this time. Initially, their goals were to gain better housing, secure fair voting rights, and end employment discrimination for Catholics in the North. Tensions mounted, and clashes with the predominantly Protestant Royal Ulster Constabulary police force became frequent. Eventually, the British Army was called in to keep the peace.

On January 30, 1972, about 10,000 people protesting internment without trial held an illegal march sponsored by the Northern Ireland Civil Rights Association. British Army barricades kept them from the center of Derry, so they marched through the Bogside neighborhood.

That afternoon, some youths rioted on the fringe of the march. An elite parachute regiment had orders to move in and make arrests in the Rossville Street area. Shooting broke out, and after 25 minutes, 13 marchers were dead and 13 were wounded (one of the wounded later died). The soldiers claimed they came under attack from gunfire and nail-bombs. The marchers said the army shot indiscriminately at unarmed civilians.

The clash, called "Bloody Sunday," uncorked pent-up frustration as moderate Nationalists morphed into staunch Republicans overnight and released a flood of fresh IRA volunteers. An investigation at the time exonerated the soldiers, but the relatives of the victims called it a whitewash and insisted on their innocence.

In 1998, then-British Prime Minister Tony Blair promised a new inquiry, which became the longest and most expensive in British legal history. In 2010, a 12-year investigation—the Saville Report—determined that the Bloody Sunday civil rights protesters were innocent and called the deaths of 14 protesters unjustified.

In a dramatic 2010 speech in the House of Commons, then-British Prime Minister David Cameron apologized to the people of Derry. "What happened on Bloody Sunday was both unjustified and unjustifiable. It was wrong," he declared. Cheers rang out in Derry's Guildhall Square, where thousands had gathered to watch the televised speech. After 38 years, Northern Ireland's bloodiest wound started healing.

ville Street toward Free Derry Corner. The murals will all be on your right.

The first mural you'll walk past is the colorful ❶ *Peace,* showing the silhouette of a dove in flight (left side of mural) and an oak leaf (right side of mural), both created from a single ribbon. A peace campaign asked Derry city schoolchildren to write suggestions for positive peacetime images; their words inspired this artwork. The dove is a traditional symbol of peace, and the oak leaf is a traditional symbol of Derry—recognized by both communities. The dove flies from the sad blue of the past toward the warm yellow of the future.

❷ *The Hunger Strikers,* repainted during the summer of 2015, features two Derry-born participants of the 1981 Maze Prison hunger strike, as well as their mothers, who sacrificed and supported them in their fatal decision (10 strikers died). The prison was closed after the release of all prisoners (both Unionist and Nationalist) in 2000.

Smaller and easy to miss (above a ramp with banisters) is ❸ *John Hume.* It's actually a collection of four faces (clockwise from upper left): Nationalist leader John Hume, Martin Luther King Jr., Nelson Mandela, and Mother Teresa. The Brooklyn Bridge in the middle symbolizes the long-term bridges of understanding that the work of these four Nobel Peace Prize-winning activists created. Born in the Bogside, Hume still maintains a home here.

Now look for ❹ *The Saturday Matinee,* which depicts an outgunned but undaunted local youth behind a screen shield. He holds

a stone, ready to throw, while a British armored vehicle approaches (echoing the famous Tiananmen Square photo of the lone Chinese man facing the tank). Why *Saturday Matinee?* It's because the weekend was the best time for locals to engage in a little "recreational rioting" and "have a go at" the army; people were off work and youths were out of school.

Nearby is ❺ *Civil Rights,* showing a marching Derry crowd carrying an anti-sectarian banner. It dates from the days when Martin Luther King Jr.'s successful nonviolent marches were being seen worldwide on TV, creating a dramatic, global ripple effect. Civil rights marches, inspired by King and using the same methods to combat a similar set of grievances, gave this long-suffering community a powerful new voice.

All along this walk you'll notice lots of flags, including the red, black, white, and green Palestinian flag. Palestinians and Catholic residents of Northern Ireland have a special empathy for each other—both are indigenous people dealing with the persistent realities of sharing what they consider their rightful homeland with more powerful settlers planted there for political reasons.

In the building behind this mural, you'll find the intense **Museum of Free Derry** (£6, £9 combo-ticket with Bogside History Tours, open Mon-Fri 9:30-16:30 year-round, also open April-Sept Sat-Sun 13:00-16:00, 55 Glenfada Park, tel. 028/7136-0880, www.museumoffreederry.org). Photos, shirts with bullet holes, and video documentary convey the experiences of the people of the Bogside during the worst of the Troubles. At the far end of the museum's outdoor wall (high up on the second floor of an adjacent residential building) is a copy of a famous painting by Francisco Goya depicting another massacre—this one in Spain—called the *Third of May 1808*. This reproduction draws a stark parallel to the local events that occurred here. Below and to the left of the painting (next to a gated alley) are two large bullet holes in the wall, inflicted on Bloody Sunday and preserved behind glass.

Cross over to the other side of Rossville Street to see the **Bloody Sunday Monument.** This small, fenced-off stone obelisk lists the names of those who died that day, most within 50 yards of this spot.

Take a look at the map pedestal by the monument, which shows how a rubble barricade was erected to block the street. A 10-story housing project called Rossville Flats stood here in those days. After peaceful protests failed (with Bloody Sunday being the watershed event), Nationalist youths became more aggressive. British troops were wary of being hit by Molotov cocktails thrown from the rooftop of the housing project.

Cross back again, this time over to the grassy median strip that runs down the middle of Rossville Street. At this end stands a granite letter *H* inscribed with the names of the 10 IRA hunger strikers who died (and how many days they starved) in the H-block of Maze Prison in 1981 (see *"The Hunger Strikers,"* earlier in the walk).

From here, as you look across at the corner of Fahan Street, you get a good view of two murals. In ❻ *The Runners* (right), three rioting youths flee tear gas from canisters used by the British Army to disperse hostile crowds. More than 1,000 canisters were used during the Battle of the Bogside; "nonlethal" rubber bullets killed 17 people over the course of the Troubles. Meanwhile, in ❼ *Operation Motorman* (left), a soldier wields a sledgehammer to break through a house door, depicting the massive push by the British

Army to open up the Bogside's barricaded "no-go" areas that the IRA had controlled for three years (1969-1972).

Walk down to the other end of the median strip where the white wall of **Free Derry Corner** announces "You are now entering Free Derry" (imitating a similarly defiant slogan of the time in once-isolated West Berlin). This was the gabled end of a string of houses that stood here more than 40 years ago. During the Troubles, it became a traditional meeting place for speakers to address crowds. A portion of this mural changes from time to time, calling attention to injustice suffered by kindred spirits around the world (the plight of Palestinians and Basques are common themes).

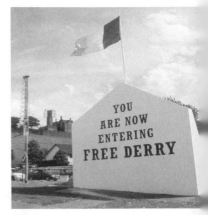

Cross back to the right side of the street (now Lecky Road) to see ❽ *Bloody Sunday,* in which a small group of men carry a body from that ill-fated march. It's based on a famous photo of Father Edward Daly that was taken that day. Hunched over, he waves a white handkerchief to request safe passage in order to evacuate a mortally wounded protester. The bloodstained civil rights banner was inserted under the soldier's feet for extra emphasis. After Bloody Sunday, the previously marginal IRA suddenly found itself swamped with bitterly determined young recruits.

Near it is a mural called ❾ *Bernadette.* The woman with the megaphone is Bernadette Devlin McAliskey, an outspoken civil rights leader, who at age 21 became the youngest elected member of British Parliament. Behind her kneels a female supporter, banging a trash-can lid against the street in a traditional expression of protest in Nationalist neighborhoods. Trash-can lids were also used to warn neighbors of the approach of British patrols.

❿ *Petrol Bomber,* showing a teen wearing an army-surplus gas mask, captures the Battle of the Bogside, when locals barricaded their community, effectively shutting out British rule. Though the main figure's face is obscured by the mask, his body clearly communicates the resolve of an oppressed people. In the background, the long-gone Rossville Flats housing project still looms, with an Irish tricolor flag flying from its top.

In ⓫ *The Death of Innocence,* a young girl stands in front of bomb wreckage. She is Annette McGavigan, a 14-year-old who was killed on this corner by crossfire in 1971. She was the 100th fatality of the Troubles, which eventually took more than 3,000

Political Murals

The dramatic and emotional murals you'll encounter in Northern Ireland will likely be one of your trip's most enduring travel memories.

During the 19th century, Protestant neighborhoods hung flags and streamers each July to commemorate the victory of King William of Orange at the Battle of the Boyne in 1690. Modern murals evolved from these colorful annual displays. With the advent of industrial paints, temporary seasonal displays became permanent territorial statements.

Unionist murals were created during the extended Home Rule political debate that eventually led to the partitioning of the island in 1921 and the creation of Northern Ireland. Murals that expressed opposing views in Nationalist Catholic neighborhoods were outlawed. The ban remained until the eruption of the modern Troubles, when staunchly Nationalist Catholic communities isolated themselves behind barricades, eluding state control and gaining freedom to express their pent-up passions. In Derry, this form of symbolic, cultural, and ideological resistance first appeared in 1969 with the simple "You are now entering Free Derry" message that you'll still see painted on the surviving gable wall at Free Derry Corner.

Found mostly in working-class neighborhoods of Belfast and Derry, today's political murals have become a dynamic form of popular culture. They blur the line between art and propaganda, giving visitors a striking glimpse of each community's history, identity, and values.

lives (and she was also a cousin of one of the artists). The broken gun beside her points to the ground, signifying that it's no longer being wielded. The large butterfly above her shoulder symbolizes the hope for peace. For years, the artists left the butterfly an empty silhouette until they felt confident that the peace process had succeeded. They finally filled in the butterfly with optimistic colors in the summer of 2006.

Finally, around the corner, you'll see a circle of male faces. This mural, painted in 1997 to observe the 25th anniversary of the tragedy, is called ⓬ *Bloody Sunday Commemoration* and shows the 14 victims. They are surrounded by a ring of 14 oak leaves—the symbol of Derry. When relatives of the dead learned that the three

Bogside Artists were beginning to paint this mural, many came forward to loan the artists precious photos of their loved ones, so they could be more accurately depicted.

Across the street, drop into the **Bogside Inn** for a beverage and check out the black-and-white photos of events in the area during the Troubles. This pub has been here through it all, and lives on to tell the tale.

While these murals preserve the struggles of the late 20th century, today sectarian violence has given way to negotiations and a settlement that seems to be working in fits and starts. The British apology for the Bloody Sunday shootings was a huge step forward. Former Nationalist leader John Hume (who shared the 1998 Nobel Peace Prize with then-Unionist leader David Trimble) once borrowed a quote from Gandhi to explain his nonviolent approach to the peace process: "An eye for an eye leaves everyone blind."

Sights in Derry

▲▲Tower Museum Derry

Occupying a modern reconstruction of a fortified medieval tower house that belonged to the local O'Doherty clan, this well-organized museum provides an excellent introduction to the city. Combining modern audiovisual displays with historical artifacts, the exhibits tell the story of the city from a skillfully unbiased viewpoint, sorting out some of the tangled historical roots of Northern Ireland's Troubles.

Cost and Hours: £4, includes audioguide for Armada exhibits, daily 10:00-17:30, last entry one hour before closing, Union Hall Place, tel. 028/7137-2411, www.derrystrabane.com/towermuseum.

Visiting the Museum: The museum is divided into two sections: the Story of Derry (on the ground floor) and the Spanish Armada (on the four floors of the tower).

Start with the **Story of Derry,** which explains the city's monastic origins 1,500 years ago. The exhibit moves through pivotal events, such as the 1688-1689 siege, as well as unexpected blips, like Amelia Earhart's emergency landing. Don't miss the thought-provoking 15-minute film in the small theater—it offers an even-handed local perspective on the tragic events of the modern sectarian conflict, giving you a better handle on what makes this unique city tick. Scan the displays of paramilitary paraphernalia in the hallway lined with colored curbstones—red, white, and blue Union Jack colors for Unionists; and the green, white, and orange Irish tricolor for Nationalists.

The tower section holds the **Spanish Armada** exhibits, filled with items taken from the wreck of *La Trinidad Valencera*. The ship sank off the coast of Donegal in 1588 in fierce storms nicknamed the "Protestant Winds." A third of the Armada's ships were lost in storms off the coasts of Ireland and Scotland. Survivors who made it ashore were hunted and killed by English soldiers. But a small number made it to Dunluce Castle, where the sympathetic lord, who was no friend of the English, smuggled them to Scotland and eventual freedom in France.

Guildhall

This Neo-Gothic building, complete with clock tower, is the ceremonial seat of city government. It first opened in 1890 on reclaimed lands that were once the mud-flats of the River Foyle. Destroyed by fire and rebuilt in 1913, it was massively damaged by IRA bombs in 1972. In an ironic twist, Gerry Doherty, one of those convicted of the bombings, was elected as a member of the Derry City Council a dozen years later. (When I first visited Derry with tour groups back in the 1990s, a bus of curious Americans was such a rarity that the mayor actually invited our entire group into his office here for tea and a friendly Q&A session.)

Cost and Hours: Free, daily 10:00-17:30, free and clean WCs on ground floor, tel. 028/7137-6510, www.derrystrabane.com/guildhall.

Visiting the Hall: Inside the hall are the Council Chamber, party offices, and an assembly hall featuring stained-glass windows showing scenes from Derry history. Take an informational pamphlet from the front window and explore, if civic and cultural events are not taking place inside. Rotating exhibits fill a ground-floor hall just to the right of the front reception desk. The Ulster Plantation exhibition is worth a visit. A mighty pipe organ fills much of a wall in the grand hall. It's lonely and loves to be played (if you play the piano and would like to give it a go, just ask a guard).

On the back terrace, facing the river, you'll find locals lunching at the pleasant Guild Café (daily 9:30-17:00). And across the street is the modest but heartfelt Peace Park, with hopeful, nonsectarian children's quotes on tiles that line the path.

Peace Bridge Stroll

A stroll across the architecturally fetching Peace Bridge rewards you with great views as you look back west over the river toward the city center. The €14 million pedestrian Peace Bridge opened in 2011, linking neighborhoods long divided by the river (Catholic Nationalists on the west bank and Protestant Unionists on the east bank). On the far side from the old city walls, the former Ebrington Barracks British Army base (1841-2003) sits on prime real estate and surrounds a huge square that was once the military parade ground. This area features a fun gastropub, and serves as an outdoor concert venue and gathering place for the community. Plans are in progress to develop this area further with a hotel and museum complex.

Hands Across the Divide

Designed by local teacher Maurice Harron, this powerful metal sculpture of two figures extending their hands to each other was

inspired by the growing hope for peace and reconciliation in Northern Ireland (located in a roundabout at the west end of Craigavon Bridge).

The Tillie and Henderson's shirt factory (opened in 1857 and burned down in 2003) once stood on the banks of the river beside the bridge, looming over the figures. In its heyday, Derry's shirt industry employed more than 15,000 workers (90 percent of whom were women) in sweathouses typical of the human toll of the Industrial Revolution. Karl Marx mentioned this factory in *Das Kapital* as an example of women's transition from domestic to industrial work lives.

St. Columb's Cathedral

Marked by the tall spire inside the walls, this Anglican cathedral was built from 1628 to 1633 in a style called "Planter's Gothic." Its construction was financed by the same London companies that backed the Protestant plantation of Londonderry. The first Protestant cathedral built in Britain after the Reformation, St. Columb's played an important part in the defense of the city during the siege. During that time, cannons were mounted on its roof, and the original spire was scavenged for lead to melt into cannon shot.

Cost and Hours: £2 donation, Mon-Sat 9:00-17:00, closed Sun, tel. 028/7126-7313, www.stcolumbscathedral.org.

Visiting the Cathedral: Before you enter, walk over to the "Heroes' Mound" at the end of the churchyard closest to the town wall. Underneath this grassy dome is a mass grave of some of those who died during the 1689 siege.

In the cathedral entryway, you'll find a hollow cannonball that was lobbed into the city—it contained the besiegers' surrender terms. Inside, along the nave, hangs a musty collection of battle flags and Union Jacks that once inspired troops during the siege, the Crimean War, and World War II. The American flag hangs among them, from the time when the first GIs to enter the European theater in World War II were based in Northern Ireland. Check out the small chapter-house museum in the back of the church to see the huge original locks of the gates of Derry and more relics of the siege.

Long Tower Church

Built below the walls on the hillside above the Bogside, this modest-looking church is worth a visit for its stunning high altar. The name comes from a stone monastic round tower that stood here for centuries but was dismantled and used for building materials in the 1600s.

Cost and Hours: Free, generally open Mon-Sat 8:30-20:30, Sun 7:30-18:00—depending on available staff and church functions, tel. 028/7126-2301, www.longtowerchurch.org.

Visiting the Church: Long Tower Church, the oldest Catholic church in Derry, was finished in 1786, during a time of enlightened relations between the city's two religious communities. Protestant Bishop Hervey gave a generous-for-the-time £200 donation and had the four Corinthian columns shipped in from Naples to frame the Neo-Renaissance altar.

Outside, walk behind the church and face the Bogside to find a simple shrine hidden beneath a hawthorn tree. It marks the spot where outlawed Masses were secretly held before this church was built, during the infamous Penal Law period of the early 1700s. Through the Penal Laws, the English attempted to weaken Catholicism's influence by banishing priests and forbidding Catholics from buying land, attending school, voting, and holding office.

Nearby: The adjacent **St. Columba Heritage Centre** fleshes out the life of Derry's patron saint and founding father (free, Mon-Fri 9:30-16:30, Sat-Sun 13:00-16:00, closed Mon Oct-April, tel. 028/7136-8491, www.stcolumbaheritage.org).

Nightlife in Derry

The **Millennium Forum** is a modern venue that reflects the city's revived investment in local culture, concerts, and plays (box office open Mon-Sat 9:30-17:00, inside city walls on Newmarket Street near Ferryquay Gate, tel. 028/7126-4455, www.millenniumforum.co.uk, boxoffice@millenniumforum.co.uk).

The **Nerve Centre** shows a wide variety of art-house films and live concerts (inside city walls at 7 Magazine Street, near Butcher Gate, tel. 028/7126-0562, www.nervecentre.org).

The **Playhouse Theatre** is an intimate venue for plays (£9-20 tickets, inside the walls on Artillery Street, between New Gate and Ferryquay Gate, tel. 028/7126-8027, www.derryplayhouse.co.uk).

To get away from tourists and mingle with Derry residents, try **Peadar O'Donnell's** pub on Waterloo Street for Derry's best nightly traditional music sessions (often start late, at 23:00; 53 Waterloo Street, tel. 028/7137-2318).

Sleeping in Derry

The first two options are located inside the city's walls and feature all the modern comforts. The others are in historic buildings with creaky charm and friendly hosts.

$$$$ Bishop's Gate Hotel is Derry's top lodging option and priced that way. A former gentlemen's club once frequented by Winston Churchill, it has 30 rooms that ooze with cushy refinement (fine bar, 24 Bishop Street, tel. 028/7114-0300, www.bishopsgatehotelderry.com, sales@bishopsgatehotelderry.com).

$$ Maldron Hotel features 93 modern and large rooms, a bistro restaurant, and 20 private basement parking spaces (Butcher Street, tel. 028/7137-1000, www.maldronhotelderry.com, info.derry@maldronhotels.com).

$ Merchant's House, on a quiet street a 10-minute stroll from Waterloo Place, is a fine Georgian townhouse with a grand, colorful drawing room and nine rooms sporting marble fireplaces and ornate plasterwork (family rooms, 16 Queen Street, tel. 028/7126-9691, www.thesaddlershouse.com, saddlershouse@btinternet.com). Joan and Peter Pyne also run the Saddler's House (see below), and offer appealing self-catering townhouse rentals inside the walls (great for families or anyone needing extra space, 3-night minimum).

$ Saddler's House, run by the owners of Merchant's House, is a charming Victorian townhouse with seven rooms located a couple of blocks closer to the old town walls. Their dog Bruno (a boxer) provides loveable comic relief (36 Great James Street, tel. 028/7126-9691, www.thesaddlershouse.com, saddlershouse@ btinternet.com).

Eating in Derry

$$$ **Entrada** is a crisp, modern restaurant with a faintly Spanish theme, serving great meals and fine wines in a posh, calm space. It faces the river a block from the Guildhall (Wed-Sat 12:00-21:30, Sun until 20:00, closed Mon-Tue, Queens Quay, tel. 028/7137-3366).

The hip, trendy $$$ **Exchange Restaurant and Wine Bar** offers lunches and quality dinners with flair, in a central location near the river behind Waterloo Place (Mon-Sat 12:00-14:30 & 17:30-22:00, Sun 16:00-21:00, Queen's Quay, tel. 028/7127-3990).

$$$ **Fitzroy's,** tucked below Ferryquay Gate and stacked with locals, serves good lunches and dinners (Mon-Sat 12:00-22:00, Sun 13:00-20:00, 2 Bridge Street, tel. 028/7126-6211).

$$ **Browns in Town** is a casual, friendly lunch or dinner option near most of my recommended lodgings (Mon-Sat 12:00-15:00 & 17:30-21:00, Sun 17:00-20:30, 21 Strand Road, tel. 028/7136-2889).

$$ **Walled City Brewery,** across the Peace Bridge, is a fun change of pace. The brewpub ambience and dependable comfort food can be washed down with a local fave: Derry chocolate milk stout (Wed-Thu 17:00-23:30, Fri-Sun from 14:00, closed Mon-Tue, 70 Ebrington Square, tel. 028/7134-3336).

$ **Mandarin Palace** is crowded with loyal locals eating filling Chinese fare; easy takeout is available (Mon-Sat 16:00-23:00, Sun from 13:00, Queens Quay, tel. 028/7137-3656).

Supermarkets: You'll find everything you need for picnics and road munchies at **Tesco** (Mon-Sat 8:00-21:00, Sun 13:00-18:00, corner of Strand Road and Clarendon Street) or **SuperValu** (Mon-Sat 8:30-19:00, Sun 12:30-17:30, Waterloo Place).

Derry Connections

From Derry, it's an hour's drive to Portrush. If you're using public transportation, consider spending £17.50 for a Zone 4 iLink smartcard (£16.50 top-up for each additional day), good for all-day train and bus use in Northern Ireland. Translink has updated schedules and prices for both trains and buses in Northern Ireland (tel. 028/9066-6630, www.translink.co.uk). Keep in mind that some bus and train schedules, road signs, and maps may say "Londonderry" or "L'Derry" instead of "Derry."

From Derry by Train to: Portrush (8/day, 1.5 hours, change in Coleraine), **Belfast** (10/day, 2.5 hours), **Dublin** (6/day, 5.5 hours, change in Belfast).

By Bus to: Galway (6/day, 5.5 hours), **Westport** (3/day, 6 hours, change in Sligo), **Portrush** (5/day, 1.5 hours, change in Coleraine), **Belfast** (hourly, 2 hours), **Dublin** (12/day, 4 hours).

Near Derry

DERRY

▲Ulster American Folk Park

This combination museum and folk park (in a wonderfully scenic and walkable rural forest) commemorates the many Irish who left their homeland during the hard times of the 18th century. Your visit progresses through four sections. You'll start by walking through the excellent museum, then head outdoors to visit the remaining three sections in chronological order: life in Ulster before emigration, passage on the boat, and the adjustment to life in unfamiliar America. You'll gain insight into the origins of the tough Scots-Irish stock—think Davy Crockett (his people were from Derry) and Andrew Jackson (Carrickfergus roots)—who later shaped America's westward migration. You'll also find good coverage of the *Titanic* tragedy, and its effect on the Ulster folk who built the ship and the loved ones it left behind.

Cost and Hours: £9; March-Sept Tue-Sun 10:00-17:00; Oct-Feb Tue-Fri 10:00-16:00, Sat-Sun 11:00-16:00; closed Mon year-round; cafeteria, 2 Mellon Road, tel. 028/8224-3292, www.nmni.com.

Getting There: The folk park is 48 kilometers (30 miles) south of Derry on A-5—about a 40-minute drive.

Nearby: The adjacent **Mellon Centre for Migration Studies** is handy for genealogy searches (Tue-Fri 10:00-16:00, Sat from 11:00, closed Sun-Mon, tel. 028/8225-6315, www.qub.ac.uk/cms).

PORTRUSH & THE ANTRIM COAST

The Antrim Coast—the north of Northern Ireland—is one of the most interesting and scenic coastlines in Ireland. Portrush, at the end of the train line, is an ideal base for exploring the highlights of the Antrim Coast. Within a few miles of the train terminal, you can visit evocative castle ruins, tour the world's oldest whiskey distillery, catch a thrill on a bouncy rope bridge, and hike along the famous Giant's Causeway.

PLANNING YOUR TIME

You need a full day to explore the Antrim Coast, so allow two nights in Portrush. With a car, you can visit the Giant's Causeway, Old Bushmills Distillery, Carrick-a-Rede Rope Bridge, and Dunluce Castle in one busy day.

On this day, get an early start. My ideal day would start with the Giant's Causeway, arriving by 9:00, when crowds are lightest; choose between a one-hour quickie visit or the scenic three-hour, five-mile "Clifftop Experience" guided hike (from Dunseverick Castle to the causeway). Early birds will find that the trails are always open.

Follow this with a tour of Old Bushmills Distillery (call ahead to reserve). For lunch, you can bring a picnic, or eat cheaply in either the visitors center at the causeway or the Old Bushmills hospitality room.

After lunch, drive to Carrick-a-Rede (about 20 minutes from the distillery). Note, though, that crossing the rope bridge now requires timed-entry tickets, which can sell out in peak season (only available same-day and assigned starting at 9:30). If tickets are sold out, you can still enjoy the scenic cliff-top trail hike all the way to the bridge, as well as the nearby viewpoint for dramatic views of the bridge. But if crossing the actual bridge is your priority, consider going to Carrick-a-Rede first thing in the morning to ensure tickets.

From here, hop in your car and double back west all the way to dramatically cliff-perched Dunluce Castle for a late-afternoon tour. The castle is only a five-minute drive from Portrush. In summer months, the long days this far north extend your sightseeing time (and most golf courses stay open until dusk).

If driving on to Belfast from Portrush, consider the slower-but-scenic coastal route via the Glens of Antrim.

GETTING AROUND THE ANTRIM COAST

By Car: A car is the best way to explore the charms of the Antrim Coast. Distances are short and parking is easy.

By Bus: In peak season, an all-day bus pass helps you get around the region economically. The **Causeway Rambler** links Portrush to Old Bushmills Distillery, the Giant's Causeway, and the Carrick-a-Rede Rope Bridge (stopping at the nearby town of Ballintoy). The bus journey from Portrush to Carrick-a-Rede takes 45 minutes (£6.50/day, runs roughly 10:00-18:00, hourly May-Sept, every two hours March-April, fewer off-season). Pick up a Rambler bus schedule at the TI, and buy the ticket from the driver (in Portrush, the Rambler stops at Dunluce Avenue, next to public WC, a 2-minute walk from TI; operated by Translink, tel. 028/9066-6630, www.translink.co.uk).

By Bus Tour: If you're based in Belfast, you can visit most of the sights on the Antrim Coast with a **McComb's** tour. Those based in Derry can get to the Giant's Causeway and Carrick-a-Rede Rope Bridge with City Sightseeing.

By Taxi: Groups (up to four) can reasonably visit most sights by taxi (except the more distant Carrick-a-Rede and Rathlin Island sailings from Ballycastle). Approximate one-way prices from Portrush: £6 (Dunluce Castle), £8 (Old Bushmills Distillery), £11 (Giant's Causeway). Try **Andy Brown's Taxi** (tel. 028/7082-2223), **Hugh's Taxi** (mobile 077-0298-6110), or **North West Taxi** (tel. 028/7082-4446).

Portrush

Homey Portrush used to be known as "the Brighton of the North." It first became a resort in the late 1800s, as railroads expanded to offer the new middle class a weekend by the shore. Victorian society believed that swimming in salt water would cure many common ailments.

This is County Antrim, the Bible Belt of Northern Ireland. When a large supermarket chain decided to stay open on Sundays, a local reverend called for a boycott of the store for not honoring the Sabbath. And in 2012, when the Giant's Causeway Visitor Centre opened, local Creationists demanded that, alongside modern geologic explanations about the age of the unique rock formations, an exhibit be added explaining their viewpoint (that, according to the Bible, the earth here was only 6,000 years old—not 60 million—carbon dating be damned).

While it's seen its best days, Portrush retains the atmosphere and architecture of a genteel seaside resort. Its peninsula is filled with lowbrow, family-oriented amusements, fun eateries and B&Bs. Summertime fun seekers promenade along the tiny harbor and tumble down to the sandy beaches, which extend in sweeping white crescents on either side.

Superficially, Portrush has the appearance of any small British seaside resort (and Union Jacks fly with a little extra gusto around here), but its history and large population of young people (students from nearby University of Ulster at Coleraine) give the town a little more personality. Along with the usual arcade amusements, there are nightclubs, restaurants, summer theater productions (July-Aug) in the town hall, and convivial pubs that attract customers all the way from Belfast.

Orientation to Portrush

Portrush's pleasant and easily walkable town center features sea views in every direction. On one side are the harbor and most of the restaurants, and on the other are Victorian townhouses and vast, salty vistas. The tip of the peninsula is filled with tennis courts, lawn-bowling greens, putting greens, and a park.

The town is busy with students during the school year. July and August are beach-resort boom time. June and September are laid-back and lazy. There's a brief but intense spike in visitors in mid-May for a huge annual motorcycle race (see "Helpful Hints," below). Families pack Portrush on Saturdays, and revelers from Belfast crowd its hotels on Saturday nights.

Tourist Information: The TI is located underneath the very central, red-brick Town Hall (July-Aug Mon-Sat 9:00-18:00, Sun from 11:00; shorter hours off-season and closed Oct-March; Kerr Street, tel. 028/7082-3333). Consider the Collins Northern Ireland Visitors Map (£5), the free *Visitor Attractions* brochure, and, if needed, a free Belfast map.

Arrival in Portrush: The train tracks stop at the base of the tiny peninsula that Portrush fills (no baggage storage at station). Most of my listed B&Bs are within a 10-minute walk of the train station. The bus stop is two blocks from the train station.

Helpful Hints: Over a four-day weekend in mid-May, thousands of die-hard motorcycle fans converge on Portrush, Port Stewart, and Coleraine to watch the Northwest 200 Race. Fearless racers scorch the roads at 200 miles per hour on the longest straightaway in motorsports. Accommodations fill up a year ahead, and traffic is the pits (dates and details at www.northwest200.org). **Causeway Laundry** offers full service (Mon-Tue and Thu-Fri 9:00-16:30, Wed and Sat until 13:00, closed Sun, 68 Causeway Street, tel. 028/7082-2060).

Sights in Portrush

Barry's Old Time Amusement Arcade
This fun arcade is bigger than it looks and offers a chance to see Northern Ireland at play. Older locals visit for the nostalgia as many of the rides and amusements go back 50 years. Prices for the various rides are listed at the door. Everything runs with tokens (£0.50 each, buy a pile from coin-op machines). Located just below the train station on the harbor, Barry's is filled with "candy floss" (cotton candy) and crazy "scoop treats" (July-Aug daily 12:30-22:00, weekends only Easter-May, closed Sept-Easter, www.barrysamusements.com).

Royal Portrush Golf Club
Irish courses, like those in Scotland, are highly sought after for their lush greens in glorious settings. Serious golfers can get a tee time at the Royal Portrush, which hosted the British Open in 1951 and is set to host it again in 2019 (green fees generally £190, less most days in off-season). Those on a budget can play the adjacent, slightly shorter Valley Course (green fees £25-£55, 10-minute walk from station, tel. 028/7082-2311, www.royalportrushgolfclub.com).

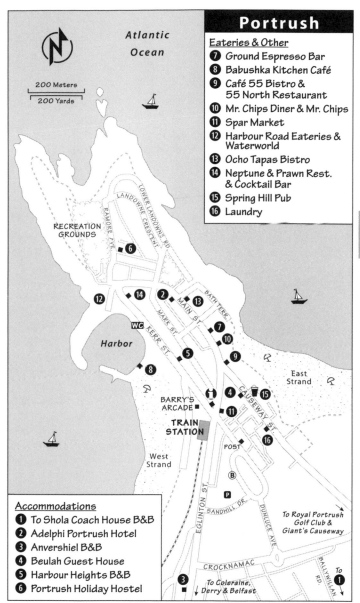

Portrush

Atlantic Ocean

200 Meters
200 Yards

Eateries & Other

- **7** Ground Espresso Bar
- **8** Babushka Kitchen Café
- **9** Café 55 Bistro & 55 North Restaurant
- **10** Mr. Chips Diner & Mr. Chips
- **11** Spar Market
- **12** Harbour Road Eateries & Waterworld
- **13** Ocho Tapas Bistro
- **14** Neptune & Prawn Rest. & Cocktail Bar
- **15** Spring Hill Pub
- **16** Laundry

PORTRUSH & ANTRIM COAST

RECREATION GROUNDS

LOWER LANDOWNE RD

LANDOWNE CRESCENT

RAMORE AVE

Harbor

WC

MARK ST

KERR ST

MAIN ST

BATH TERR.

BATH ST

East Strand

BARRY'S ARCADE

TRAIN STATION

West Strand

CAUSEWAY ST

POST

EGLINTON ST

SANDHILL DR

DUNLUCE AVE

CROCKNAMAC

BALLYWILLAN RD

To Royal Portrush Golf Club & Giant's Causeway

To Coleraine, Derry & Belfast

To 1

Accommodations

- **1** To Shola Coach House B&B
- **2** Adelphi Portrush Hotel
- **3** Anvershiel B&B
- **4** Beulah Guest House
- **5** Harbour Heights B&B
- **6** Portrush Holiday Hostel

Portrush Recreation Grounds

For some easygoing exercise right in town, this well-organized park offers lawn-bowling greens (£5/hour with gear), putting greens, tennis courts, and a great kids' play park. You can rent tennis shoes, balls, and rackets, all for £10/hour (Mon-Sat 10:00-dusk, Sun from 12:00, closed mid-Sept-May, tel. 028/7082-4441).

Waterworld

For more fun, consider Waterworld, with pools, waterslides, and bowling (£5, Mon-Sat 10:30-18:00, Sun from 12:00, closed Sept-May; wedged between Harbour Bistro and Ramore Wine Bar, tel. 028/7082-2001).

Sleeping in Portrush

Portrush has a range of hotels, from depressing to ritzy. Some B&Bs can be well-worn. August and Saturday nights can be tight (and loud) with young party groups. Otherwise, it's a "you take half a loaf when you can get it" town. Rates vary with the view and season—probe for softness. Many listings face the sea, though sea views are worth paying for only if you get a bay window. Ask for a big room (some doubles can be very small; twins are bigger). Lounges are invariably grand and have bay-window views. Most places listed have lots of stairs. All but Shola Coach House are perfectly central and within a few minutes' walk of the train station. Parking is easy.

$$$ Shola Coach House is a memorable treat that exceeds other B&B experiences in Northern Ireland. About 1.5 miles south of town, it's easiest for drivers (otherwise it's a 30-minute uphill walk or £5 taxi ride). The secluded, 170-year-old, renovated stone structure once housed the coaches and horses for a local land-lord. The decor of the four rooms is tasteful, the garden patio is delightful, and Sharon and David Schindler keep it spotless (parking, no kids under 18, 2-night minimum, 110A Gateside Road at top of Ballywillan Road, tel. 028/7082-5925, mobile 075-6542-7738, www.sholabandb.com, sholabandb@gmail.com).

$$$ Adelphi Portrush is a breath of fresh air, with 28 tastefully furnished modern rooms, an ideal location, friendly staff, and a hearty bistro downstairs (family rooms, 67 Main Street, tel. 028/7082-5544, www.adelphiportrush.com, stay@adelphiportrush.com).

$ Anvershiel B&B, with seven nicely refurbished rooms, is a great value (RS%, family rooms, parking, 10-minute walk south of train station, 16 Coleraine Road, tel. 028/7082-3861, www.anvershiel.com, enquiries@anvershiel.com, Alan and Janice Thompson).

$ Beulah Guest House is a traditional, old-fashioned place. It's centrally located and run by cheerful Helen and Charlene McLaughlin, with 11 prim rooms (parking at rear, 16 Causeway Street, tel. 028/7082-2413, www.beulahguesthouse.com, stay@ beulahguesthouse.com).

$ Harbour Heights B&B rents nine retro-homey rooms, each named after a different town in County Antrim. It has an inviting guest lounge, supervised by two tabby cats, overlooking the harbor. Friendly South African hosts Sam and Tim Swart—a photographer—manage the place with a light hand (family rooms, 17 Kerr Street, tel. 028/7082-2765, mobile 078-9586-6534, www. harbourheightsportrush.com, info@harbourheightsportrush.com).

¢ Portrush Holiday Hostel offers clean, well-organized, economical lodging for bottom-feeding vagabonds (private rooms available, tel. 028/7082-1288, mobile 078-5037-7367, 24 Princess Street, www.portrushholidayhostel.com, info@portrushholidayhostel.com).

Eating in Portrush

As a family getaway from Belfast and a beach escape for students from the nearby university in Coleraine, Portrush has more than enough fish-and-chips joints. And in recent years, the refined tastes of affluent golfers and urban professionals out for a weekend has prompted the town to up its culinary game.

LUNCH SPOTS

$ Ground Espresso Bar makes fresh sandwiches and *panini,* soup, and great coffee (daily July-Aug 9:00-22:00, Sept-June until 17:00, 52 Main Street, tel. 028/7082-5979).

$ Babushka Kitchen Café serves fresh sandwiches and creative desserts with an unbeatable view—actually out on the pier (daily 9:15-17:00, West Strand Promenade, tel. 077-8750-2012).

$$ Café 55 Bistro serves basic sandwiches with a great patio view (daily 9:00-17:00, longer hours in summer, shorter hours off-season, 1 Causeway Street, beneath fancier 55 North restaurant, tel. 028/7082-2811).

$ Mr. Chips Diner and **Mr. Chips** are the local favorites for cheap, quality fish-and-chips (daily 12:00-22:00, 12 and 20 Main Street). Both are mostly takeout while the diner also has tables. The smaller Mr. Chips cooks with lard (less healthy, more traditional). The bigger Mr. Chips cooks with vegetable oil (healthier) and hangs the stars and bars of the Confederate flag on the wall (when it comes to the Catholic/Protestant issue, this is a conservative town with some redneck tendencies).

Groceries: For picnic ingredients, try **Spar Market** (daily

7:00-20:00, June-Aug until 23:00, across from Barry's Arcade on Main Street, tel. 028/7082-5447).

HARBOUR ROAD EATERIES

A creative, diverse, and lively quintet of restaurants clusters together overlooking the harbor. With the same owner, they all have a creative and fun energy, are often jammed with diners, and are basically open nightly from 17:00 to 22:00 (exceptions noted below). All are described at RamoreRestaurant.com (only the Mermaid Kitchen & Bar takes reservations).

$$ Ramore Wine Bar is a salty, modern place, with an inviting menu ranging from steaks to vegetarian food. It's very casual but with serious cuisine. Order at the bar and take a table (also open for lunch, tel. 028/7082-4313).

$$ Coast Pizzeria is a hit for its pizza, pasta, and burgers. It's noisy and youthful with tight seating (tel. 028/7082-3311).

$$$ Harbour Bistro is dark, noisy, and sprawling with a sloppy crowd enjoying chargrilled meat and fish (tel. 028/7082-2430).

$$ Mermaid Kitchen & Bar is all about fresh fish dishes with a Spanish twist and great harbor views. Those at the bar get a bird's-eye view of the fun banter and precision teamwork of the kitchen staff (closed Mon-Tue, tel. 028/7082-6969).

$$$ Neptune & Prawn (just across the inlet from the others) is the most yacht-clubby of the bunch. Serving Asian and other international food, with a fancy presentation and many plates designed to be shared, this place is noisy and high-energy, with rock music playing (tel. 028/7082-2448).

OTHER DINING OPTIONS OFF THE HARBOR

$$$ 55 North (named for the local latitude) has the best sea views in town, with windows on three sides. The filling pasta-and-fish dishes, along with some Asian plates, are a joy. Their lunch and early-bird special (order by 18:45) is three courses at the cost of the entrée (daily 12:30-14:00 & 17:00-21:00, 1 Causeway Street, tel. 028/7082-2811).

$$ Ocho Tapas Bistro brings sunny Spanish cuisine to the chilly north, featuring a great early-bird menu—choose any three tapas from a varied list (Tue-Fri 17:00-21:30, Sat-Sun 12:30-14:30 and 17:00-22:00, closed Mon, 92 Main Street, tel. 028/7082-4110).

PUBS

Harbour Bar is an old-fashioned pub next to the Harbour Bistro (see listing above). **Harbour Gin Bar** (above Harbour Bar) is romantic and classy—a rustic, spacious, and inviting place with live acoustic folk music from 20:30 (almost nightly) and a fun selection of 45 gins.

Neptune & Prawn Cocktail Bar (above the restaurant by the same name; see listing earlier) has great views over the harbor and is the most classy-yet-inviting place in town for a drink.

Spring Hill Pub is also a good bet for its friendly vibe and occasional live music (17 Causeway Street, tel. 028/7082-3361).

Portrush Connections

Consider a £17.50 Zone 4 iLink smartcard, good for all-day Translink train and bus use in Northern Ireland (£16.50 top-up for each additional day). Translink's website has updated schedules and prices for both trains and buses in Northern Ireland (tel. 028/9066-6630, www.translink.co.uk).

From Portrush by Train to: Coleraine (hourly, 12 minutes), **Belfast** (15/day, 2 hours, transfer in Coleraine), **Dublin** (7/day, 5 hours, transfer in Coleraine or Belfast). Note that on Sundays, service is greatly reduced.

By Bus to: Belfast (12/day, 2 hours; scenic coastal route, 2.5 hours), **Dublin** (4/day, 5.5 hours).

Antrim Coast

The craggy 20-mile stretch of the Antrim Coast extending eastward from Portrush to Ballycastle rates second only to the tip of the Dingle Peninsula as the prettiest chunk of coastal Ireland. From your base in Portrush, you have a varied grab bag of sightseeing choices: Giant's Causeway, Old Bushmills Distillery, Dunluce Castle, Carrick-a-Rede Rope Bridge, and Rathlin Island.

It's easy to weave these sights together by car, but connections are patchy by public transportation. Bus service is viable only in summer, and taxi fares are reasonable only for the sights closest to Portrush (Dunluce Castle, Old Bushmills Distillery, and the Giant's Causeway). For details on how to plan your day on the Antrim Coast, and for more on your transportation options, see "Planning Your Time" and "Getting Around the Antrim Coast," at the beginning of this chapter.

PORTRUSH & ANTRIM COAST

The Scottish Connection

The Romans called the Irish the "Scoti" (meaning pirates). When the Scoti crossed the narrow Irish Sea and invaded the land of the Picts 1,500 years ago, that region became known as Scoti-land. Ireland and Scotland were never conquered by the Romans, and they retained similar clannish Celtic traits. Both share the same Gaelic branch of the linguistic tree.

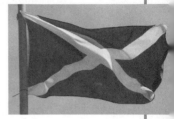

On clear summer days from Carrick-a-Rede, the island of Mull in Scotland—only 17 miles away—is visible. Much closer on the horizon is the boomerang-shaped Rathlin Island, part of Northern Ireland. Rathlin is where Scottish leader Robert the Bruce (a compatriot of William "Braveheart" Wallace) retreated in 1307 after defeat at the hands of the English. Legend has it that he hid in a cave on the island, where he observed a spider patiently rebuilding its web each time a breeze knocked it down. Inspired by the spider's perseverance, Robert gathered his Scottish forces once more and finally defeated the English at the decisive Battle of Bannockburn.

Flush with confidence from his victory, Robert the Bruce decided to open a second front against the English...in Ireland. In 1315, he sent his brother Edward over to enlist their Celtic Irish cousins in an effort to thwart the English. After securing Ireland, Edward hoped to move on and enlist the Welsh, thus cornering England with their pan-Celtic nation. But Edward's timing was bad—Ireland was in the midst of famine. His Scottish troops had to live off the land and began to take food and supplies from the starving Irish. He might also have been trying to destroy Ireland's crops to keep them from being used as a colonial "breadbasket" to feed English troops. The Scots quickly wore out their welcome, and Edward the Bruce was eventually killed in battle near Dundalk in 1318.

This was the first time in history that Ireland was used as a pawn by England's enemies. Spain and France saw Ireland as the English Achilles' heel, and both countries later attempted invasions of the island. The English Tudor and Stuart royalty countered these threats in the 16th and 17th centuries by starting the "plantation" of loyal subjects in Ireland. The only successful long-term settlement by the English was here in Northern Ireland, which remains part of the United Kingdom today.

It's interesting to imagine how things might be different today if Ireland and Scotland had been permanently welded together as a nation 700 years ago. You'll notice the strong Scottish influence in this part of Ireland when you ask a local a question and he answers, "Aye, a wee bit." The Irish joke that the Scots are just Irish people who couldn't swim home.

Sights on the Antrim Coast

▲▲Giant's Causeway

This five-mile-long stretch of coastline is famous for its bizarre basalt columns. The shore is covered with largely hexagonal pillars that stick up at various heights. It's as if the earth were offering God a choice of 37,000 six-sided cigarettes.

Geologists claim the Giant's Causeway was formed by volcanic eruptions more than 60 million years ago. As the surface of the lava flow quickly cooled, it contracted and crystallized into columns (resembling the caked mud at the bottom of a dried-up lakebed, but with far deeper cracks). As the rock later settled and eroded, the columns broke off into the many stair-like steps that now honeycomb the Antrim Coast.

Of course, in actuality, the Giant's Causeway was made by a giant Ulster warrior named Finn MacCool who knew of a rival giant living across the water in Scotland. Finn built a stone bridge over to Scotland to spy on his rival, and found out that the Scottish giant was much bigger. Finn retreated back to Ireland and had his wife dress him as a sleeping infant, just in time for the rival giant to come across the causeway to spy on Finn. The rival, shocked at the infant's size, fled back to Scotland in terror of whomever had sired this giant baby. Breathing a sigh of relief, Finn tore off the baby clothes and prudently knocked down the bridge. Today, proof of this encounter exists in the geologic formation that still extends undersea and surfaces in Scotland (at the island of Staffa).

Cost and Hours: The Giant's Causeway is free and open all the time. But in practice, anyone parking there needs to pay £10.50, which includes an audioguide (or guided walk) and entrance to the visitors center (daily 9:00-18:00, July-Aug until 19:00, Nov-April until 17:00, tel. 028/2073-1855, www.nationaltrust.org. uk/giantscauseway). A gift shop and café are in the visitors center.

Visiting the Causeway: For cute variations on the Finn story, as well as details on the ridiculous theories of modern geologists, start in the **Giant's Causeway Visitor Centre.** It's filled with kid-friendly interactive exhibits giving a worthwhile history of the Giant's Causeway, with a regional overview. On the far wall opposite the entrance, check out the interesting three-minute video showing the evolution of the causeway from molten lava to the geometric, geologic wonderland of today. The large 3-D model of the causeway

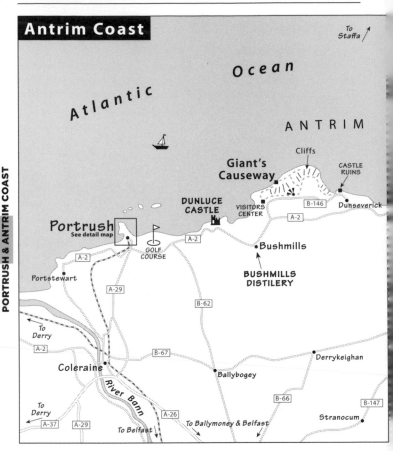

offers a bird's-eye view of the region. There's also an exhibit about the history of tourism here from the 18th century.

The **causeway** itself is the highlight of the entire coast. The audioguide (included with the visitors center ticket) highlights 15 stops along the causeway, each with a photo of the formation being described; all stops are shown on the map you'll receive with your ticket. (Your admission also includes a one-hour guided walk—leaving regularly with demand—covering the same information as the audioguide.)

From the visitors center, you have several options for visiting the causeway:

Short and Easy: A **shuttle bus** (4/hour from 9:00, £1 each way) zips tired tourists a half-mile from the visitors center down a paved road to the causeway. This standard route (the blue dashed line on your map) offers the easiest access and follows the stops on your audioguide. Many choose to walk down and then take the shuttle back up.

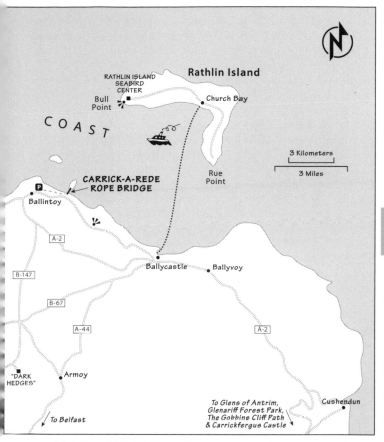

Mid-Level Hike: For a longer hike and a more varied dose of causeway views, consider the cliff-top trail (red dashed line on your map). Take the easy-to-follow trail uphill from the visitors center 10 minutes to Weir's Snout, the great fence-protected precipice viewpoint. Then hike 15 minutes farther (level) to reach the Shepherd's Steps. Then grab the banister on the steep (and slippery-when-wet) stairs that zigzag down the switchbacks toward the water. At the T-junction, go 100 yards right, to the towering rock pipes of "the Organ." (You can detour another 500 yards east around the headland, but the trail dead-ends there.) Now retrace your steps west on the trail (don't go up the steps again), continuing down to the tidal zone, where the "Giant's Boot" (6-foot boulder, on the right) provides some photo fun. Another 100 yards farther is the dramatic point where the causeway meets the sea. Just beyond that, at the asphalt turnaround, is the shuttle bus stop.

Just below the bus stop is a fine place to explore the uneven, wave-splashed rock terraces, watching your every easy-to-trip step. Look for "wishing coins"—rusted and bent—that have been jammed into the cracks of rock just behind the turnaround (where the trail passes through a notch in the 20-foot-high rock wall).

Return to the visitors center by hiking up the paved lane (listening to the audioguide at stops along the way). Or, from the turnaround, you can catch the shuttle bus back to the visitors center (just line up and pay the driver).

Longer Hike: Hardy hikers and avid photographers can join the guided three-hour **Clifftop Experience** trek exploring the trail that runs along a five-mile section of the Causeway Coast, starting at the meager ruins of Dunseverick Castle (yellow dashed line on your map). Operated by the National Trust, the hike is led by a naturalist, who ventures beyond the usual big-bus tourist crowds to explore the rugged rim of this most-scenic section of the Antrim Coast. Expect undulating grass and gravel paths with no WC options and no shelter whatsoever from bad weather (£30, daily at 10:30, must prebook, no kids under 12, catch 5-minute ride on bus #402 from visitors center to Dunseverick trailhead, tel. 028/2073-3419, www.giantscausewaytickets.com, northcoastbookings@nationaltrust.org.uk).

This same hike could also be done on your own. Occasional rock falls and slides can close this trail (ask first at Portrush TI, or call ahead to visitors center). If going independently, a good plan is to take the Causeway Rambler bus (see "Getting Around the Antrim Coast," earlier) or a taxi from Portrush to Dunseverick Castle (east of Giant's Causeway on B-146). Get off there and hike west, following the cliff-hugging contours of Benbane Head back to the visitors center. You'll have a fence on your left and the cliff on the right, so there's no doubt about the route. When you're finished, travel back to Portrush by taxi or Rambler bus (check bus schedules ahead of time at Portrush TI or at www.translink.co.uk). For more info on hiking the route without a naturalist, see www.visitcausewaycoastandglens.com and search for "North Antrim Cliff Path."

▲▲Old Bushmills Distillery

Bushmills claims to be the world's oldest distillery. Though King James I (of Bible translation fame) only granted Bushmills its license to distill "Aqua Vitae" in 1608, whiskey has been made here since the 13th century. Distillery tours waft you through the process, making it clear that Irish whiskey is triple distilled—and therefore smoother than Scotch whisky (distilled merely twice and minus the "e").

Cost and Hours: £8 for 45-minute tour followed by a tasting; tours go on the half-hour Mon-Sat 9:30-16:00 (last tour), Sun from 12:00; Nov-March tours run Mon-Sat 10:00-15:30 (last tour), Sun from 12:00; tours are limited to 30 people and book

For *Game of Thrones* Fans

Even if you don't give a bloody Stark about the *Game of Thrones* TV saga, you'll notice references to it as you travel around Northern Ireland. Much of the series is filmed here, both on location and in the Titanic Quarter studio in Belfast. Other scenes are shot in Croatia, Spain, Morocco, and Iceland, but the cast is subjected most often to Irish weather. An average visit to the Antrim Coast is a traipse through the set: Dragonstone, the Stormlands, and the Iron Islands were brought to life along the same route that travelers use to see Dunluce Castle and Carrick-a-Rede Rope Bridge. For those who are truly interested in the approach of a very long winter, there are several options: both McComb's (www.mccombscoaches.com; see page 64) and Game of Thrones Tours (www.gameofthronestours.com) run £40 day tours from Belfast to various spots in the seven kingdoms.

With a car, use the map at www.discovernorthernireland.com/GameofThrones to find filming locations. Without leaving County Antrim, you can visit Ballintoy Harbour (Stormlands), Larrybane (Iron Islands), Murlough Bay (Storm's End), and the Dark Hedges (King's Road) with no more than an hour's driving time. Just avoid any re-enactments, as the nearest major hospital that treats dragon burns is in Belfast.

up—reserve ahead in summer; note that in July, you can still tour, but the distillery machinery is shut down for annual maintenance; tel. 028/2073-3218, www.bushmills.com.

Visiting the Distillery: Tours start with the mash pit, which is filled with a porridge that eventually becomes whiskey. (The leftovers of that porridge are fed to the county's particularly happy cows.) Bushmills is made of only three ingredients: malted barley, water, and yeast. You'll see a huge room full of whiskey aging in oak casks—casks already used to make bourbon, sherry, and port. Whiskey picks up its color and personality from this wood (which breathes and has an effective life of 30 years). Bushmills shapes the flavor of its whiskey by carefully finessing the aging process—often in a mix of these casks.

To see the distillery at its lively best, visit when the 100 workers are staffing the machinery—Monday morning through Friday noon. (The still is still on weekends and in July.) The finale, of course, is the opportunity for a sip in the 1608 Bar—the former malt barn. Visitors get a single glass of their choice. Hot-drink enthusiasts might enjoy a cinnamon-and-cloves hot toddy. Teetotalers can just order tea. After the tour, you can get a decent lunch in the hospitality room.

Warning to Shoppers: Customs allowance is one liter per person, which the distillery cannot ship home. To bring some home, you must pack it in your checked bag (pad it well and put it in a plastic bag in case it leaks; airlines will not accept liability for bottles breaking).

Nearby: The distillery is just outside of **Bushmills town,** which is a loyalist festival of red, white, and blue flags and bunting. Banners posted throughout the town celebrate illustrious Ulster men and women and people far and wide with Ulster heritage (like Mark Twain and Dolly Parton).

▲▲Carrick-a-Rede Rope Bridge

For 200 years, fishermen hung a narrow, 90-foot-high bridge (planks strung between wires) across a 65-foot-wide chasm between the mainland and a tiny island. Today, the bridge (while not the original version) gives access to the sea stack where salmon nets were set (until 2002) during summer months to catch the fish turning and hugging the coast's corner. (The complicated system is described at the gateway.) A pleasant, 30-minute, one-mile walk from the parking lot takes you down to the rope bridge. Cross over to the island for fine views and great seabird-watching, especially during nesting season. A coffee shop and WCs are near the parking lot.

Cost and Hours: £7 trail and bridge fee; daily 9:30-18:00, July-Aug until 19:00, Nov-Feb until 15:30; last entry 45 minutes before closing, tel. 028/2076-9839, www.nationaltrust.org.uk.

Timed-Entry Tickets: Due to a record number of visitors in 2016, timed tickets are now required to cross the bridge. Arrive as early as possible; they sell only 240 tickets (same-day only) for each hour-long entry window. If you arrive on a busy day, you may have to wait an hour or even find that all the day's tickets are sold. Cruise groups and big buses arrive after 11:00. (If you're frustrated at the ticket booth, you're welcome to hike down to the bridge for free but won't be able to venture onto it.)

Nearby Viewpoint: If you have a car and a picnic lunch, don't miss the terrific coastal scenic rest area one mile steeply uphill and east of Carrick-a-Rede (on B-15 to Ballycastle). This grassy area offers one of the best picnic views in Northern Ireland (tables but no WCs). Feast on bird's-eye views of the rope bridge, nearby Rathlin Island, and the not-so-distant Island of Mull in Scotland.

▲Dunluce Castle

These romantic ruins, perched dramatically on the edge of a rocky headland, are a testimony to this region's turbulent past. During the Middle Ages, the castle was a prized fortification. But on a stormy night in 1639, dinner was interrupted as half of the kitchen fell into the sea, taking the servants with it. That was the last straw for the lady of the castle. The countess of Antrim packed up and moved inland, and the castle "began its slow submission to the forces of nature."

Cost and Hours: £5, daily 10:00-17:00, winter until 16:00, tel. 028/2073-1938.

Visiting the Castle: While it's one of the largest castles in Northern Ireland and is beautifully situated, there's precious little left to see among Dunluce's broken walls.

Before entering, catch the eight-minute video about the history of the castle (across from the ticket desk). The ruins themselves are dotted with plaques that show interesting artists' renditions of how the place would have looked 400 years ago.

The 16th-century expansion of the castle was financed by treasure salvaged from a shipwreck. In 1588, the Spanish Armada's *Girona*—overloaded with sailors and the valuables of three abandoned sister ships—sank on her way home after the aborted mission against England. More than 1,300 drowned, and only five survivors washed ashore. The shipwreck was more fully excavated in 1967, and a bounty of golden odds and silver ends wound up in Belfast's Ulster Museum.

Rathlin Island

The only inhabited island off the coast of Northern Ireland, Rathlin is a quiet haven for hikers, birdwatchers, and seal spotters. Less than seven miles from end to end, this "L"-shaped island is reachable by ferry from the town of Ballycastle.

Getting There: The Rathlin Island passenger-only ferry departs from Ballycastle, just east of Carrick-a-Rede (10 trips per day in summer). Six are fast 25-minute trips, and four are slower 45-minute trips (£12 round-trip per passenger, smart to prebook, as the ferry can sell out on summer days; tel. 028/2076-9299, www.rathlinballycastleferry.com).

Travelers with rental cars park in Ballycastle (only special-permit holders can take a car onto the ferry). A taxi from Portrush to Ballycastle runs £25 one-way. Bus service from Portrush to Ballycastle is spotty (check with the TI in Portrush, or contact Translink—tel. 028/9066-6630, www.translink.co.uk).

Visiting Rathlin Island: Rathlin's population of 110 islanders clusters around the ferry dock at Church Bay. Here you'll find the **Rathlin Boathouse Visitor Centre,** which operates as the island's TI (daily 10:00-12:30 & 13:00-17:00, closed in winter, on the bay 100 yards east of the ferry dock, mobile 077-0886-9605).

In summer, a shuttle bus (£5 round-trip) meets arriving ferries and drives visitors to the **Rathlin Island Seabird Centre** at the west end of the island. Entry to the Seabird Centre (£5) includes a tour of its unique lighthouse, extending down the cliff with its beacon at the bottom. It's upside-down because the coast guard wants the light visible only from a certain distance out to sea. The bird observation terrace at the center (next to the lighthouse) overlooks one of the most dramatic coastal views in Ireland—a sheer drop of more than 300 feet to craggy sea stacks just offshore that are draped in thousands of seabirds. Bring your most powerful zoom lens for photos.

Rathlin has seen its fair share of history. Flint ax heads were quarried here in Neolithic times. The island was one of the first in Ireland to be raided by Vikings, in 795. Robert the Bruce hid out from English pursuers on Rathlin in the early 1300s (see "The Scottish Connection" sidebar, earlier). In the late 1500s, local warlord Sorely Boy MacDonnell stashed his extended family on Rathlin and waited on the mainland at Dunluce Castle to face his English enemies...only to watch in horror as they headed for the island instead to massacre his loved ones. And in 1917, a WWI U-boat sank the British cruiser HMS *Drake* in Church Bay. The wreck is now a popular scuba-dive destination, 60 feet below the surface.

▲Antrim Mountains and Glens

Not particularly high (never more than 1,500 feet), the Antrim Mountains are cut by a series of large glens running northeast to the sea. Glenariff, with its waterfalls—especially the Mare's Tail—is the most beautiful of the nine glens (described next). Travelers going by car can take a pleasant drive from Portrush to Belfast, sticking to the (more scenic but less direct) A-2 road that stays near the coast and takes in parts of all the Glens of Antrim.

▲Glenariff Forest Park

Glenariff Forest Park offers scenic picnic spots and hiking trails as well as a cozy tea shop. The parking lot alone has a lovely view down the glen to the sea. You'll find more spectacular scenery on the two-mile waterfall trail along the river gorge, while an easygoing half-mile stroll on the viewpoint trail via the ornamental gardens also provides lovely views (£5 parking fee, daily 10:00-

dusk, trail map available at café onsite, tel. 028/7034-0870, www. nidirect.gov.uk).

Getting There: The entry is off A-43 (via A-26; eight miles south of Cushendall, follow signs).

Nearby: Continue along the A-2 scenic coastal route and take a short jog up to Cushendall, where there's a nice beach for a picnic, or just head south on A-2 toward the Gobbins Cliff Path and the castle at Carrickfergus (see listings in the Belfast chapter).

BELFAST

Seventeenth-century Belfast was just a village. With the influx, or "plantation," of English and (more often) Scottish settlers, the character of the place changed. After the Scots and English were brought in—and the native Irish were subjugated—Belfast blossomed, spurred by the success of the local linen, rope-making, and especially shipbuilding industries. The Industrial Revolution took root here with a vengeance. While the rest of Ireland remained rural and agricultural, Belfast earned its nickname ("Old Smoke") during the time when many of the brick buildings that you'll see today were built. The year 1888 marked the birth of modern Belfast. After Queen Victoria granted city status to this boomtown of 300,000, its citizens built Belfast's centerpiece, City Hall.

Belfast is the birthplace of the *Titanic* (and many other ships that didn't sink). In 2012, to mark the 100th anniversary of the *Titanic* disaster, a modern new attraction was launched in Belfast's shipyard, telling the ill-fated ship's fascinating and tragic story. Nearby, two huge, mustard-colored cranes (built in the 1970s, and once the biggest in the world, nicknamed Samson and Goliath) rise like skyscrapers. They stand idle now, but serve as a reminder of this town's former shipbuilding might...strategic enough to be the target of four Luftwaffe bombing raids in World War II.

At the beginning of the 21st century, the peace process (substantially defusing the sectarian Troubles) began to take root, and investments from south of the border—the Republic of Ireland—injected quiet optimism into the dejected shipyards where the *Titanic* was built. Like everywhere else in Ireland, the 2008 economic crash gave investors a sobering lesson. But Belfast officials have

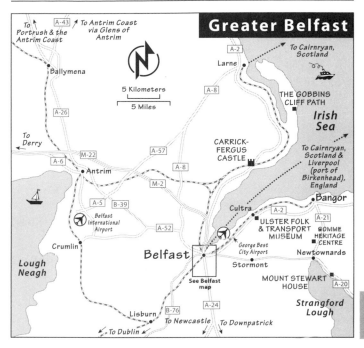

Greater Belfast

To Portrush & the Antrim Coast

To Antrim Coast via Glens of Antrim

A-43

Ballymena

5 Kilometers

5 Miles

A-2

Larne

To Cairnryan, Scotland

THE GOBBINS CLIFF PATH

A-8

A-26

Irish Sea

To Derry

CARRICK-FERGUS CASTLE

A-57

M-22

A-6

Antrim

A-8

To Cairnryan, Scotland & Liverpool (port of Birkenhead), England

M-2

Bangor

A-5

B-39

Belfast International Airport

A-52

Cultra

A-2

A-21

ULSTER FOLK & TRANSPORT MUSEUM

SOMME HERITAGE CENTRE

Crumlin

Belfast

George Best City Airport

Newtownards

Lough Neagh

See Belfast map

Stormont

MOUNT STEWART HOUSE

A-20

Lisburn

B-76

A-24

Strangford Lough

To Dublin

To Newcastle

To Downpatrick

BELFAST

resumed hope that the historic Titanic Quarter will continue to attract development...and lots of tourists.

It feels like a new morning in Belfast. A forest of cranes stand sentinel over numerous building sites. The skyline is changing rapidly, especially along the once depressing Lagan riverfront. It's hard to believe that the bright and bustling pedestrian center was once a subdued, traffic-free security zone. There's no longer any hint of security checks, once a tiresome daily routine. These days, both Catholics and Protestants root for the Belfast Giants ice hockey team. And aggressive sectarian murals are slowly being repainted with scenes celebrating heritage pride...less carnage, more culture.

Still, it's a fragile peace. Hateful bonfires, built a month before they're actually set ablaze, still scorch the pavement each July. Pubs with security gates are reminders that the island is still split—and 900,000 Protestant Unionists in the North prefer it that way.

PLANNING YOUR TIME

Big Belfast is thin on sights. For most, one day of sightseeing is plenty. But I've also included advice for longer stays.

Day Trip from Dublin

Using the handy, two-hour Dublin-Belfast train (about €40 for "day return" tickets), you could make Belfast a day trip:

7:35	Catch the train from Dublin's Connolly Station (arriving in Belfast's Central Station at 9:45; confirm train times)
11:00	Take the City Hall tour (12:00 on Sat-Sun), browse the pedestrian zone, have lunch, and ride a shared black taxi up Falls Road
15:00	Visit Titanic Belfast (after midday crowds subside) or side-trip to the Ulster Folk Park and Transport Museum in nearby Cultra (closed Mon)
Evening	Return to Dublin (last train departs Belfast Mon-Sat at 21:30 and arrives in Dublin at 23:45)

Note about Sundays: Trains depart later and return earlier on this day, compressing your already limited sightseeing time (first train departs Dublin at 10:00 and arrives in Belfast at 12:08; last train departs Belfast at 19:05 and pulls into Dublin at 21:15).

Staying Overnight

Belfast makes a pleasant overnight stop, with plenty of cheap hostels, reasonable B&Bs, weekend hotel deals, and a relaxed neighborhood full of B&Bs 30 minutes away in Bangor.

Two Days in Belfast: On the first day, follow my day-trip itinerary described earlier. For your second day, take the City Sightseeing bus tour in the morning, then visit Carrickfergus Castle in the afternoon.

Two Days in Small-Town Northern Ireland: From Dublin (via Belfast), take the train to Portrush; allow two nights and a day to tour the Causeway Coast (castle, whiskey distilleries, Giant's Causeway, resort fun), then follow the Belfast-in-a-day plan described earlier. With a third day, add Derry.

Coming from Scotland or England: With cheap flights from Edinburgh or Glasgow, as well as slow ferry connections (from Cairnryan in Scotland or Liverpool in England; see "Belfast Connections," later), it's easy to begin your exploration of the Emerald Isle in Belfast, and then head south to Dublin and the Republic.

Orientation to Belfast

Belfast is flat and spread out, with the following zones of interest: **Titanic Quarter** (northeast of city center; docklands with Odyssey entertainment complex and Titanic Belfast), **western Belfast** (working-class sectarian neighborhoods west of A-12 freeway), **city center** (Donegall Square, City Hall, pedestrian shopping, TI), **Cathedral Quarter** (north of City Hall; Ulster-Scots Centre, Northern Ireland War Memorial, lively nightlife), and **southern Belfast** (Botanic Gardens, Queen's University, Ulster Museum).

The eastern part of Belfast is more affluent and residential, with little of interest to the average sightseer, except for Stormont (the seat of government in Northern Ireland).

The modern bookends of sightseeing interest are the Titanic Belfast attraction (in the Titanic Quarter to the north) and the Lyric Theatre (near the university district to the south). Their contemporary angularities are hard to miss, as they contrast sharply with the red-brick uniformity of old Belfast. But the core of your city navigating will hinge on four more central landmarks (listed from north to south): St. Anne's Cathedral, City Hall, Shaftesbury Square, and Queen's University. Find them on your map, and use them to navigate as you stroll the town.

Belfast's "Golden Mile" commercial drag—stretching from Hotel Europa to the university district—connects the central and southern zones with some of the best dinner and entertainment spots.

TOURIST INFORMATION

The modern TI (look for *Visit Belfast* sign) has a courteous staff and baggage storage (£3.50/bag for 4 hours, £5/bag for 8 hours; Mon-Sat 9:00-17:30, June-Sept until 19:00, Sun 11:00-16:00 year-round; a couple of doors down from the Linen Hall Library, just across Chichester Street, north of City Hall at 9 Donegall Square North, tel. 028/9024-6609, http://visitbelfast.com). City walking tours depart from the TI (see "Tours in Belfast," later). Pick up a free copy of *Visit Belfast*, which lists all the sightseeing and evening entertainment options.

ARRIVAL IN BELFAST

By Train: Arriving by train, you'll go directly to Belfast's Central Station (with an ATM in the lobby). From the station, a free Centrelink bus loops to Donegall Square, with stops near Shaftesbury Square (recommended hostel), the bus station (some recommended hotels), and the TI (free with any train or bus ticket, 4/hour, none on Sun; during morning rush hour, bus runs only between station and Donegall Square). Allow about £5 for a taxi from Central Station to Donegall Square, or £8 to my accommodation listings south of the university.

Slower trains arc through the city, stopping at several downtown stations, including Central Station, Great Victoria Station (most central, near Donegall Square and most hotels), and Botanic Station (close to the university, Botanic Gardens, and some recommended lodgings). It's easy and cheap to connect stations by train (£1.50).

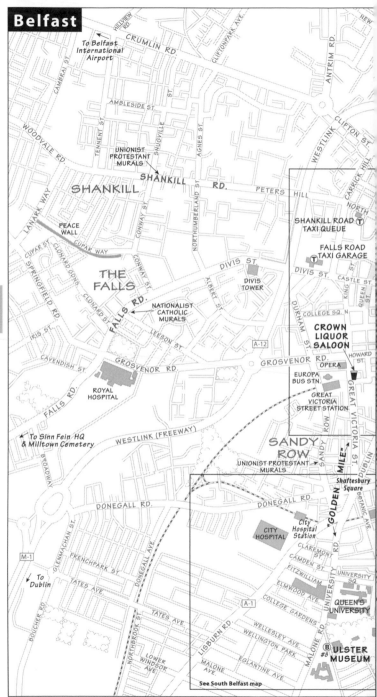

Belfast

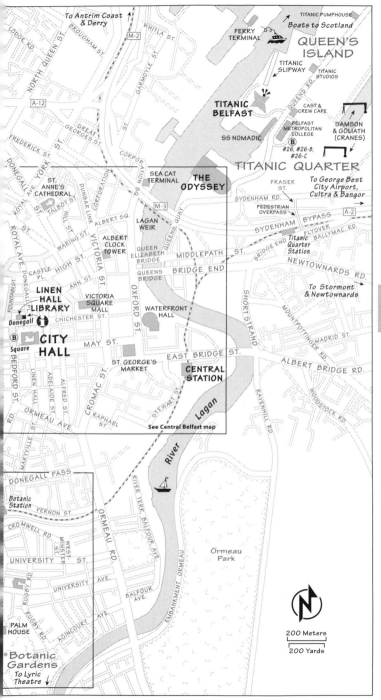

See Central Belfast map

BELFAST

By Car: Driving in Belfast, although not as bad as in Dublin, is still a pain. Avoid it if possible. Street parking in the city center is geared for short stops (use pay-and-display machines, £0.30/15 minutes, one-hour maximum, Mon-Sat 8:00-18:00, free in evenings and on Sun).

HELPFUL HINTS

Belfast Visitor Pass: This pass combines iLink smartcards for free bus and rail travel, with sightseeing discounts, for one day or two or three consecutive days within the Belfast Visitor Pass Zone (all of downtown Belfast as far out as the Ulster Folk and Transport Museum in Cultra, but not as far as Carrickfergus or Bangor). The handy one-day pass saves money for anyone visiting Titanic Belfast (10 percent discount) and the Ulster Folk and Transport Museum (30 percent discount) while connecting them by train or bus (free with pass). Buy it at the TI, any train station, either airport, Europa Bus station, or online (£6.50 for 1-day pass, £11 for 2 days, £14.50 for 3 days, tel. 028/9066-6630, www.translink.co.uk).

Market: On Friday, Saturday, and Sunday, the Victorian confines of **St. George's Market** is a commotion of commerce and a people-watching delight. Friday is a variety market (6:00-14:00), Saturday blooms with food and garden items (9:00-15:00), and Sunday creaks with crafts and antiques (10:00-16:00). It's located at the corner of Oxford and East Bridge streets (5 blocks east of Donegall Square, tel. 028/9043-5704, www.belfastcity.gov.uk/markets).

Shopping Mall: Victoria Square is a glitzy American-style mall. Its huge glass dome reflects Belfast's economic rejuvenation. For fine city views, ride the free elevator to the observation platform high up inside the dome (Mon-Sat 9:30-18:00, Wed-Fri until 21:00, Sun 13:00-18:00; 3 blocks east of City Hall—bordered by Chichester, Victoria, Ann, and Montgomery streets; www.victoriasquare.com).

Post Office: The main post office, with lots of fun postcards, is at the intersection of High and Bridge streets (Mon-Fri 9:00-17:30, Sat until 12:30, closed Sun, 3 long blocks north of Donegall Square).

Services: Located directly across University Road from the red-brick university building, **Queen's University Student Union** is just as handy for tourists as it is for college students. Inside you'll find an ATM, WCs, a minimarket, and Wi-Fi. Grab a quick and cheap sandwich and coffee at **Clement's Coffee Shop** (long hours Mon-Sat, closed Sun).

Laundry: Globe Launderers has both self-serve and drop-off service (Mon-Fri 8:00-21:00, Sat until 18:00, Sun 12:00-18:00,

37 Botanic Avenue, tel. 028/9024-3956). For the hotel neighborhood south of the university, the closest is **Whistle Cleaners** (drop-off service, Mon-Fri 8:30-18:00, Sat 9:00-17:30, closed Sun, 160 Lisburn Road, at intersection with Eglantine Avenue, tel. 028/9038-1297).

Bike Rental: Belfast Bike Tours rents bikes only if reserved in advance (£15/day, daily but no set hours, off Wellington Park behind Wellington Park Hotel, mobile 078-1211-4235, www.belfastbiketours.com).

GETTING AROUND BELFAST

If you line up your sightseeing logically, you can do most of this flat town on foot. On wheels, you have several options. For most visitors, the Belfast Visitor Pass will save time and money. It combines iLink smartcards for local bus and train trips with sightseeing discounts (see "Helpful Hints," earlier).

By Train or Bus: Ask about iLink smartcards, which give individuals one day of unlimited train and bus travel. The Zone 1 card (£6.50) covers the city center, Cultra (Ulster Folk Park and Transport Museum), and George Best Belfast City Airport. The handy Zone 2 card (£11) includes Bangor and Carrickfergus Castle. The Zone 3 card (£14.50) is really only useful for reaching Belfast's distant international airport. Zone 4 (£17.50) gets you anywhere in Northern Ireland, including Portrush and Derry (£16.50 top-up for each additional day). For those lingering in the North, one-week cards offer even better deals. Buy your iLink card at any train station in the city.

If you're traveling from Belfast to only one destination—Carrickfergus Castle, Cultra, or Bangor—a "day return" ticket is cheaper than two one-way tickets.

Pink-and-white city buses go from Donegall Square East to Malone Road and my recommended accommodations (any #8 bus, 3/hour, £2, all-day pass costs £4 Mon-Sat before 9:30—after 9:30 and on Sun it's £3.70). Sunday service is much less frequent.

For more information on iLink smartcards, trains, and buses in Belfast, contact Translink (tel. 028/9066-6630, www.translink.co.uk).

By Taxi: Taxis are reasonable and a good option. For general transport, as opposed to the taxi tours described later, try **Valu Cabs** (tel. 028/9080-9080). Cabs charge a flat £3 rate for any ride (£3.40 from 22:00 to 6:00) and £2 per mile after that. If you're going up Falls Road, ride a shared cab (explained later, under "Sights in Belfast").

Tours in Belfast

ON FOOT
▲General Walking Tours

Belfast Compass Tours introduces you to the city's 300-year history on a balanced two-hour stroll. Highlights include City Hall, St. George's Market, Albert Clock, and the opulent Merchant Hotel (£7, must book in advance, mobile 079-4425-6560 or 079-3440-7751, www.belfastcompasstours.com).

Belfast Hidden Tours focuses on the culture of North Belfast, going heavier on trade and industry with a sprinkling of rebel sedition and Luftwaffe destruction, while leading visitors to less obvious "hidden" corners of the city (£10, March-Oct daily at 10:00, 12:00, and 14:00, no 10:00 tour on Sun, meet at Visit Belfast TI, tel. 079-7189-5746, www.belfasthiddentours.com).

Belfast Trad Trail Tours hosts this musical pub crawl. It's led by two local musicians, who walk you between three fun drinking establishments, and play and explain traditional Irish music at each pub. It's a great intro to Irish music and the pulsing evening scene of the Cathedral Quarter. It starts at 16:00 and lasts about 2.5 hours, allowing you time afterward to dine and explore the neighborhood (£15, mid-May-Aug daily at 16:00, meet at Dirty Onion Pub, 3 Hill Street, tel. 028/9028-8818, www.tradtrail.com).

Local Guides

Susie Millar is a sharp former BBC TV reporter who thrives on showing visitors around her native Belfast. With family connections to the *Titanic* tragedy, she knows that sad, yet inspiring chapter inside and out. She can also take you farther afield by car (yours or hers) when she is not busy guiding Rick Steves tours (£25/person for half-day tour, book in advance, mobile 078-5271-6655, www.titanictours-belfast.co.uk, info@titanictours-belfast.co.uk).

Lynn Corken is a friendly, knowledgeable, and flexible Jill-of-all-trades, with a passion for her hometown. She's willing to customize her guiding to your interests (on foot or with her car) when she's not on the road leading Rick Steves tours (£100/half-day, £200/day, book in advance, mobile 077-7910-2448, lynncorken@hotmail.co.uk).

Sectarian Neighborhoods Walking Tours

Two walking tours offer opposite viewpoints on the Troubles and local culture. Listen and learn. Or, as an Irish friend once told me, "Never give unsolicited advice...wise men don't need it and fools won't heed it."

Coiste Irish Political Tours offers the Nationalist/Republican perspective on extended, two-hour walks along Falls Road. Led by former IRA prisoners, you'll visit murals, gardens of remembrance, peace walls, and community centers in this slowly rejuvenating section of gritty Belfast. Tours meet beside the Divis Tower (the 20-story apartment house at the east end of the Divis Road near the A-12 Westlink motorway overpass) and end at the Milltown Cemetery (£10; Tue, Thu, and Sat at 11:00, Sun at 14:00; best to book in advance, tel. 028/9020-0770, www.coiste.ie).

Sandy Row Walking Tours provides the Unionist/Loyalist point of view during its 1.5-hour walks centering on Sandy Row, Belfast's oldest residential neighborhood. Tours cover the city's industrial heritage, the Orange Order, both World Wars, and historic local churches. They depart from the King William Mural at the intersection of Sandy Row and Linfield Road (£7.50; daily at 10:00, 14:00, and 17:00; best to book in advance, mobile 079-0925-4849, www.historicsandyrow.co.uk).

ON WHEELS

▲Hop-On, Hop-Off Bus Tours

City Sightseeing offers the best quick introduction to the city's political and social history. Their open-top, double-decker buses link major sights and landmarks, including the Catholic and Protestant working-class neighborhoods, the Stormont Parliament building, Titanic Belfast, and City Hall, with commentary on political murals and places of interest. The route also has convenient stops near several lodging options listed later: Fisherwick Place (Jurys Inn), Shaftsbury Square (Benedicts Hotel and Belfast International City Hostel), and Malone Road (Malone Lodge and Wellington Park Hotel). Pay cash on bus or book online in advance (£12.50 for 48 hours, 2/hour, fewer in winter, daily 10:00-16:00, 20 stops, 1.5-hour loop; departs from Castle Place on High Street, 2 blocks west of Albert Clock Tower; tel. 028/9032-1321, http://belfastcitysightseeing.com).

City Tours offers a route with more than 20 stops. It starts on High Street (near Albert Clock), then veers westward to take in Falls and Shankill roads (£10 for 48 hours, runs 2/hour 9:45-16:45, pay cash on bus or book in advance, tel. 028/9032-1912, www.citytoursbelfast.com).

Sectarian Taxi Tours

This is the easiest way to view the evolving murals of the Catholic and Protestant communities with a local who has lived through the events that inspired them. In recent years, these taxi tours have begun venturing onto each other's turf to give a more balanced, yet still opinionated personal perspective. Their unscripted commentary is as varied as their individual personalities. See "Sectarian Neighborhoods in West Belfast," later, for details on Falls and Shankill roads.

Avoid squeezing more than four passengers into a cab because the views from the middle seats are restricted. However, drivers are willing to stop (where traffic allows) to let you out for photos.

Taxi Trax Black Taxi Tours—from a Nationalist Catholic area—gives 90-minute **Falls Road**-based tours (£35/1-3 people, £12/additional person, cheap for small groups, at the intersection of Castle and King streets in Castle Junction Car Park, tel. 028/9031-5777 or mobile 078-9271-6660, www.taxitrax.com).

NI Black Taxi Tours—from a Unionist Protestant area—takes you on 90-minute tours around **Shankill Road** (£30/1-3 people, £10/additional person, cheap for small groups, book in advance, mobile 077-2968-3104, www.niblacktaxitours.com).

Bike Tours

Belfast Bike Tours offers 2.5-hour rides in the countryside south of town. Departing from the front gate of Queen's University, you'll pedal along an old canal towpath to the Giant's Ring (ancient dolmen) and back on generally flat terrain (£15; April-Aug Mon, Wed, Fri-Sat at 10:30 and 14:00; Sept-March Sat 10:30 and 14:00; bikes, helmets, and bottle of water provided; must reserve ahead by phone or email, mobile 078-1211-4235, www.belfastbiketours.com, info@belfastbiketours.com).

Minibus Tours

McComb's Giant's Causeway Tour visits Carrickfergus Castle, the Giant's Causeway, Dunluce Castle (photo stop only), Carrick-a-Rede Rope Bridge, and Old Bushmills Distillery (£25, doesn't include distillery admission, daily depending on demand, book through and depart from the recommended Belfast International City Hostel, pickup around 9:00, back to Belfast by 19:00). Their *Game of Thrones* tour visits many of the sites where the hit fantasy TV series was filmed (£35, starts around 8:30, back to Belfast by 19:00). They also have private guides (book in advance, tel. 028/9031-5333, www.mccombscoaches.com).

BY BOAT
Titanic Tours

The **Lagan Boat Company** shows you shipyards on this one-hour cruise, narrated by a member of the Belfast Titanic Society. The tour shows off the fruits of the city's £800 million investment in its harbor, including a weir built to control the tides and stabilize the depth of the harbor (it doubles as a free

pedestrian bridge over the River Lagan). The heart of the tour is a lazy harbor cruise past rusty dry-dock gates, brought alive by the guide's proud commentary and passed-around historical photos (£10; April-Oct daily sailings at 12:30, 14:00, and 15:30; fewer off-season, tel. 028/9024-0124, www.laganboatcompany.com). Tours depart from the Lagan Pedestrian Bridge and Weir on Donegall Quay. The quay is located just past the leaning Albert Clock Tower, a 10-minute walk from the TI.

Sights in Belfast

TITANIC QUARTER

Up until the mid-1990s, this district was a barren wasteland of cement slabs and rusting industrial relics. But during the Celtic Tiger boom years (which spilled over into the North), shrewd investors saw the real estate potential and began building posh, high-rise condos.

The first landmark project to be completed was the Odyssey entertainment complex (in 2000). To draw more visitors and commemorate the proud shipbuilding industry of the Victorian and Edwardian Ages, another flagship attraction was needed. The 100th anniversary of the *Titanic* disaster in 2012 provided the perfect opportunity, and the result is the Titanic Belfast.

The Odyssey

This huge millennium-project complex offers a food pavilion, bowling alley, and W5 science center with interactive, educational exhibits for youngsters. Where else can a kid play a harp with laser-light strings? The "W5" stands for "who, what, when, where, and why" (£9.80, kids-£6.50, Mon-Fri 10:00-17:00, Sat until 18:00, Sun 12:00-18:00, last entry one hour before closing, 2 Queen's Quay, 10-minute walk north of Belfast's Central Station, tel. 028/9046-7790, www.w5online.co.uk).

There's also a 12-screen cinema and the 11,000-seat SSE Odyssey Arena, where the Belfast Giants professional hockey team skates from September to March on Friday or Saturday nights (£16 game tickets, tel. 028/9073-9074, www.belfastgiants.com).

▲▲▲Titanic Belfast

This £97 million attraction stands right next to the original slipways where the *Titanic* was built. Creative displays tell the tale of the famous ocean liner, proudly heralded as the largest man-made moving object of its time. The sight has no actual artifacts from the underwater wreck (out of respect for the fact that it's a mass grave). The artifacts on display are from local shipbuilding offices and personal collections.

Cost and Hours: £18; daily April-Sept 9:00-18:00, June-Aug

BELFAST

Belfast at a Glance

▲▲▲**Titanic Belfast** Excellent but crowded high-tech exhibit covering the famously infamous ship and local shipbuilding, housed in a stunning structure on the site where the *Titanic* was built. **Hours:** Daily April-Sept 9:00-18:00, June-Aug until 19:00; Oct-March 10:00-17:00. See page 65.

▲▲ **Sectarian Neighborhoods Taxi Tours** Local cabbies drive visitors through West Belfast's Falls Road and Shankill Road neighborhoods, offering personal perspectives on the slowly fading Troubles. See page 69.

▲▲**City Hall** Central Belfast's polished and majestic celebration of Victorian-era pride built with industrial wealth. **Hours:** Daily 8:30-17:00. See page 71.

▲**Ulster Museum** Mixed bag of local artifacts, natural history, and coverage of political events; a good rainy-day option near Queen's University. **Hours:** Tue-Sun 10:00-17:00, closed Mon. See page 75.

▲**Botanic Gardens** Belfast's best green space, featuring the Palm House loaded with delicate tropical vegetation. **Hours:** Daily 8:00 until dusk; Palm House open daily 10:00-17:00, Oct-March until 16:00. See page 76.

Near Belfast

▲▲**Ulster Folk Park and Transport Museum** A glimpse into Northern Ireland's hard-working heritage, split between a charming re-creation of past rural life and halls of innovative vehicular advances (8 miles east of Belfast). **Hours:** March-Sept Tue-Sun 10:00-17:00; Oct-Feb Tue-Fri 10:00-16:00, Sat-Sun 11:00-16:00; closed Mon year-round. See page 76.

▲**Carrickfergus Castle** Northern Ireland's first and most important fortified refuge for invading 12th-century Normans (14 miles northeast of Belfast). **Hours:** Daily 10:00-17:00, Oct-March until 16:00. See page 78.

▲**The Gobbins** Rugged, unique, wave-splashed hiking trail cut into coastal rock, accessible by guided tour (34 miles northeast of Belfast). **Hours:** Visitor center daily 9:30-17:30, guided hikes about every hour in good weather. See page 78.

Near Bangor

▲**Mount Stewart House** Fine 18th-century manor house displaying ruling-class affluence, surrounded by lush and calming gardens (18 miles east of Belfast). **Hours:** Daily 10:00-16:30, closed Nov-Feb. See page 88.

BELFAST

until 19:00; Oct-March 10:00-17:00; last admission about 90 minutes before closing (though the Late Saver Ticket is sold one hour before closing for £9); audioguide-£3, but you get plenty of info without it; located on Queen's Island, tel. 028/9076-6399, www. titanicbelfast.com.

Crowd-Beating Tips: Go early or late as big bus-tour or cruise-ship crowds can clog the exhibits from 10:00 to 14:00. Book ahead online to get the entry time you want.

Getting There: From Donegall Square, take bus #26 or #26B (both stop behind Belfast Metropolitan College, infrequent buses on Sun), or go by taxi (£6 ride). The Titanic Quarter train station is a 15-minute walk to the south of the Titanic Belfast.

Tours: The **Discovery Tour** explains the striking architecture of the Titanic Belfast building and the adjacent slipways where the ship was built (£8.50, 1 hour, call ahead for tour times).

Eating: The ground floor includes a **$ Galley Express** (sandwich café) as well as **$$ Bistro 401** (a carvery-style restaurant). Or, walk one block east (away from the tourist crowds), through the arch in the Drawing Offices building and across Queens Road to the battleship-gray **$$ Cast & Crew** for a sandwich, soup, or salad (daily 12:00-18:00).

Visiting the Sight: The spacey architecture of the Titanic Belfast building is a landmark on the city's skyline. Six stories tall, it's clad in more than 3,000 sun-reflecting aluminum panels. Its four corners represent the bows of the many ships (most of which didn't sink) that were built in these yards during the industrial Golden Age of Belfast.

The exhibit's nine galleries are numbered differently than the floors, but it doesn't matter as you'll be routed on a one-way path through six floors. If you have any questions, there are helpful "crew" everywhere you look.

The "shipyard ride" near the beginning is a fun (if cheesy) five-minute experience. Six people share a gondola as you glide through a series of vignettes that attempt to capture what it was like to be a worker building the ship. (There can be a 20-minute wait—if strapped for time, I'd skip it and use that time more productively in the fascinating displays that follow.)

Continuing on, you'll find a big window overlooking the actual construction site (which you'll visit after leaving the building). Next, you'll see exhibits on the construction, historic photographs, proud displays of the opulence on board, the disaster (with Morse code transmissions sent after the ship hit the iceberg) and, in the

200-seat Discovery Theatre, the seven-minute *Titanic Beneath* video, with eerie footage of the actual wreckage sprouting countless "rusticles" 12,000 feet down on the ocean floor. Don't miss the see-through floor panels at the foot of the movie screen where the wreck passes slowly under your feet.

The last escalator leaves you on the ground floor facing the back door of the center. Step outside. Just beyond the door, in the pavement, is a big, stylized map showing the route of the *Titanic's* one and only voyage. The brown benches are long and short—set up in dots and dashes to represent the Morse code distress transmissions sent on that fateful day. Just beyond two dashes, a few steps to the left, find the symbolic steel tip of the ship in the pavement and stand there looking out. This was where the bow was; the lampposts (stretching 300 yards before you) mark the size of the ship built here. Fifty yards ahead is a memorial with the names of all who perished.

Nearby: The SS *Nomadic* tender ship, which once ferried passengers between the dock and the *Titanic*, is docked 50 yards south of Titanic Belfast and easily visible (included with Titanic Belfast ticket, same hours as Titanic Belfast).

Thompson Dry Dock and Pump-House

Those with an unsinkable interest in the *Titanic* may want to walk down into the massive footprint where it last rested on dry land, to get a feel for how colossal the vessel was. The pump house filled the dry dock with water—and emptied it—in record time. Slipways rolled hulls down a slope into the water, where they were then towed to a dry dock. It's here that the final outfitting was completed, adding extra weight before the final watertight launch. Standing on the floor of this humongous concrete bathtub is humbling, especially when looking at the well-placed historic photos that show how snugly the ship fit here.

Cost and Hours: £3, daily 10:30-16:00, www.titanicsdock.com.

Getting There: From the Titanic Belfast, it's a 15-minute walk north to the Dry Dock and Pump-House. En route, you'll pass the huge **Titanic Studios** building, where interiors of *Game of Thrones* and *City of Ember* were filmed.

SECTARIAN NEIGHBORHOODS IN WEST BELFAST

It will be a happy day when the sectarian neighborhoods of Belfast have nothing to be sectarian about. For a look at three of the original home bases of the Troubles, explore the working-class neighborhoods of Catholic Falls Road and Protestant Shankill Road (west of the Westlink motorway), or Protestant Sandy Row (south of the Westlink motorway).

Murals (found in working-class, sectarian areas) are a memorable part of any visit to Belfast. But with more peaceful times, the character of these murals is slowly changing. The Re-Imaging Communities Program has spent £3 million in government money to replace aggressive murals with positive ones. Paramilitary themes are gradually being covered over with images of pride in each neighborhood's culture. The *Titanic* was built primarily by proud Protestant Ulster stock and is often seen in their neighborhood murals—reflecting their industrious work ethic. Over in the Catholic neighborhoods, you'll see more murals depicting mythological heroes from the days before the English came.

Hop-on, hop-off bus tours regularly drive these roads. But taxi tours of Falls Road or Shankill Road are more interactive (quiz the cabbie, who grew up here) and allow you to pull over to take photos.

▲▲Falls Road (Catholic)

At the intersection of Castle and King streets, you'll find the Castle Junction Car Park. On the ground floor of this nine-story parking garage, a passenger terminal (entrance on King Street) connects travelers with old black cabs—and the only Irish-language signs in downtown Belfast. These shared black cabs efficiently shuttle residents from outlying neighborhoods up and down Falls Road and to the city center. This service originated almost 50 years ago at the beginning of the Troubles, when locals would hijack city buses and use them as barricades in the street fighting. When bus service was discontinued, local sectarian groups established the shared taxi service. Although the buses are now running again, these cab rides are still a great value for their drivers' commentaries.

Any cab goes up Falls Road, past Sinn Fein headquarters and lots of murals, to the Milltown Cemetery (£6, sit in front and talk

to the cabbie). Hop in and out. Easy-to-flag-down cabs run every minute or so in each direction on Falls Road. Or, take a one-hour tour from a trained black-taxi cabbie.

Visiting Falls Road: The Sinn Fein office and bookstore are near the bottom of Falls Road. The **bookstore** is worth a look. Page through books featuring color photos of the political murals that decorated these buildings. Money raised here supports the families of deceased IRA members.

A sad, corrugated structure called the **peace wall** runs a block

or so north of Falls Road (along Cupar Way), separating the Catholics from the Protestants in the Shankill Road area. The first cement wall was 20 feet high—it was later extended another 10 feet by a solid metal addition, and then another 15 feet with a metal screen. Seemingly high enough now to deter a projectile being lobbed over, this is one of many such walls erected in Belfast during the Troubles. Meant to be temporary, these barriers stay up because of old fears among the communities on both sides. In 2013, the Northern Ireland Assembly announced its ambitious goal to remove all of these walls by 2023, but a lack of resources and weak community unity have resulted in little progress.

At the **Milltown Cemetery,** walk past all the Gaelic crosses down to the far right-hand corner (closest to the highway), where

little green railings set apart the IRA Roll of Honor from the thousands of other graves. These martyrs are treated like fallen soldiers. Notice the memorial to Bobby Sands and nine other hunger strikers. They starved themselves to death in the nearby Maze Prison in 1981, protesting for political prisoner status as opposed to terrorist criminal treatment. Maze Prison closed in the fall of 2000.

Shankill Road and Sandy Row (Protestant)

A shared black cab brings you though the Shankill Road area, but an easier and cheaper way to get a dose of the Unionist side is to walk **Sandy Row.** From Hotel Europa, walk a block down Glen-

gall Street, then turn left for a 10-minute walk along a working-class Protestant street. A stop in a Unionist memorabilia shop, a pub, or one of the many cheap eateries here may give you an opportunity to talk to a local. You'll see murals filled with Unionist symbolism. The mural of William of Orange's victory over the Catholic King James II (Battle of the Boyne, 1690) thrills Unionist hearts. You'll find it at the northern end of Sandy Row at the corner with Linfield Road.

CENTRAL BELFAST
▲▲City Hall

This grand structure's 173-foot-tall copper dome dominates the town center. Built between 1898 and 1906, with its statue of Queen Victoria scowling down Belfast's main drag and the Neoclassical dome looming behind her, the City Hall is a stirring sight. Take a close look at the Queen Victoria monument and how it celebrates the industrial might of Belfast: shipping, linen (the woman with the bobbin), and education (the student). Facing the building, if you go around to the left, you'll find the Titanic Memorial Garden.

Cost and Hours: Free, daily 8:30-17:00; handy Bobbin coffee shop on ground floor, tel. 028/9032-0202, www.belfastcity.gov.uk/cityhall.

Tours: Free 45-minute tours of City Hall run Mon-Fri at 10:00, 11:00, 14:00, 15:00, and 16:00; Sat-Sun at 12:00, 14:00, 15:00, and 16:00 (fewer off-season); call or check online to confirm schedule.

Visiting City Hall: If you can't manage a tour, at least step into the main lobby to admire the marble-swirl staircase and the view up into the dome. In 1912, at the center of the marble floor design beneath the dome, Sir Edward Carson signed the Ulster Covenant—to be followed by 470,000 other Unionists at dozens of desks surrounding City Hall that day. Some signed with their own blood. The Covenant stated Unionists would use "all means necessary" (including the might of the 100,000-strong UVF militia) to resist the Home Rule bill that had just passed in Parliament. The bill would have given the entire island of Ireland limited autonomy from Britain. These Protestant Unionists did not want this new level of political distance from Britain and feared that "Home Rule is Rome Rule." They would have become the minority in a more independent Catholic Ireland. World War I interrupted the implementation of Home Rule, and the partition of Ireland followed shortly after the war's end.

Belfast History and Culture Exhibit: A worthwhile, 16-room exhibit fills the ground floor of City Hall. It covers the history of the city, culture, industry, the WWII bombings, and the Troubles (free, open same hours as the building).

Linen Hall Library

Across the street from City Hall, the 200-year-old Linen Hall Library welcomes guests (notice the red hand above the front door

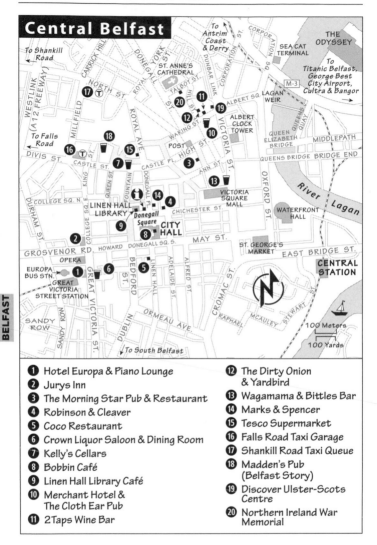

Central Belfast

1 Hotel Europa & Piano Lounge
2 Jurys Inn
3 The Morning Star Pub & Restaurant
4 Robinson & Cleaver
5 Coco Restaurant
6 Crown Liquor Saloon & Dining Room
7 Kelly's Cellars
8 Bobbin Café
9 Linen Hall Library Café
10 Merchant Hotel & The Cloth Ear Pub
11 2 Taps Wine Bar
12 The Dirty Onion & Yardbird
13 Wagamama & Bittles Bar
14 Marks & Spencer
15 Tesco Supermarket
16 Falls Road Taxi Garage
17 Shankill Road Taxi Queue
18 Madden's Pub (Belfast Story)
19 Discover Ulster-Scots Centre
20 Northern Ireland War Memorial

facing Donegall Square North). Described as "Ulster's attic," the library takes pride in being a neutral space where anyone trying to make sense of the sectarian conflict can view the Troubled Images, a historical collection of engrossing political posters. It has a fine hardbound ambience, a coffee shop (nice light lunches), and a royal newspaper reading room. Climb to the top floor and then go down the back staircase, where the walls are lined with fascinating original posters from those tough times.

Cost and Hours: Free; Mon-Fri 9:30-17:30, Sat until 16:00, closed Sun; 45-minute tours for £5—daily at 11:30, 17 Donegall Square North, tel. 028/9032-1707, www.linenhall.com.

Golden Mile

This is the overstated nickname of Belfast's liveliest dining and entertainment district, which stretches from the Opera House (Great Victoria Street) to the university (University Road).

The **Grand Opera House,** originally built in 1895, bombed and rebuilt in 1991, and bombed and rebuilt again in 1993, is extravagantly Victorian and *the* place to take in a concert, play, or opera (ticket office open Mon-Sat 10:00-17:30, closed Sun; ticket office to right of main front door on Great Victoria Street, tel. 028/9024-1919, www.goh.co.uk). The recommended **Hotel Europa,** next door, while considered to be the most-bombed hotel in the world (33 times during the Troubles), actually feels pretty casual (but is expensive).

Across the street is the museum-like **Crown Liquor Saloon.** Built in 1849, it's now a part of the National Trust. A wander through its mahogany, glass, and marble interior is a trip back into the days of Queen Victoria, although the privacy provided by the snugs—booths—allows for un-Victorian behavior (consider a lunch stop—see "Eating in Belfast," later). Upstairs, the Crown Dining Room serves pub grub and is decorated with historic photos.

CATHEDRAL QUARTER

This rejuvenating district is about a 15-minute walk north of City Hall, in the oldest part of the city. You'll find an unexpected cluster of culture that will make you rethink your preconceptions about Belfast. Besides being home to the following sights, it's a memorable maze for a wander, where mind-bending murals put the "fun" in "funky" and show the artistic alternative to the sectarian murals found elsewhere. For the best scene, head for the intersection of Hill Street and Commercial Court and peek into nearby breezeways. It's also a good place for a lively dinner.

Discover Ulster-Scots Centre

This bright and inviting gallery is designed to promote the Ulster-Scots heritage. Ulster and Scotland are 13 miles apart, and this exhibit feels almost like propaganda, trying to make it clear that the first Scots were from northeastern Ireland and the cultures are rightfully intertwined. If your heritage is Scots-Irish (as they be-

1916

This pivotal year means vastly different things to Northern Ireland's two communities. When you say "1776" to most Americans, it means revolution and independence from tyranny (unless, perhaps, you're a Native American). But when you say "1916" to someone in Northern Ireland, the response depends on who's talking.

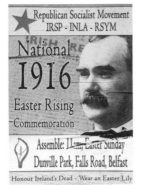

To Nationalists (who are usually Catholic), "1916" brings to mind the Easter Rising—which took place in Dublin in April of that year and was the beginning of the end of 750 years of British rule for most of Ireland. Some Nationalist murals still use images of Dublin's rebel headquarters or martyred leaders like Patrick Pearse and James Connolly. To this community, 1916 emphasizes their proud Gaelic identity, their willingness to fight to preserve it, and their stubborn anti-British attitude.

To Unionists (who are usually Protestant), "1916" means the brutal WWI Battle of the Somme in France, which began that July. (For more on the Somme, visit the Somme Heritage Centre in Bangor, described on page 89.) Although both Catholic and Protestant soldiers died in this long and bloody battle, the first wave of young men who went over the top were the sons of proud Ulster Unionists. The Unionists hoped this sacrifice would prove their loyalty to the Crown—and assurance that the British would never let them be gobbled up by an Irish Nationalist state (a possible scenario just before the Great War's outbreak). You'll see Tommies heroically climbing out of their trenches in some of Belfast's Unionist murals. For the Unionists, 1916 is synonymous with devout, almost righteously divine, Britishness.

came known in America) this is the place to begin your genealogy research.

Cost and Hours: Free, Mon-Fri 10:00-16:00, closed Sat-Sun, one block from clock tower at 1 Victoria Street, tel. 028/9043-6710, http://discoverulsterscots.com.

BELFAST

Northern Ireland War Memorial

This one-room sanctuary is dedicated to the lives lived and lost in this corner of the U.K. during World War II. Coverage includes the American troops based here during the war and the damage done by multiple German bombing raids during the Blitz.

Cost and Hours: Free, Mon-Fri 10:00-16:30, closed Sat-Sun, 21 Talbot Street, tel. 028/9032-0392, www.niwarmemorial.org.

St. Anne's Cathedral

Also known as Belfast Cathedral, this Anglican church was built in the early 1900s, at the peak of Belfast's industrial power. The novel spire is a spike like the one so famous in Dublin. Goofy nicknames are a passion throughout Ireland: This one's dubbed "the Rod to God."

Cost and Hours: £5, Mon-Sat 9:00-17:00, evensong on Sun at 15:30, Donegall Street, tel. 028/9032-8332.

SOUTH BELFAST
▲Ulster Museum

This is Belfast's most venerable museum. It offers an earnest and occasionally thought-provoking look at the region's history, with a cross-section of local artifacts.

Cost and Hours: £3 suggested donation; Tue-Sun 10:00-17:00, closed Mon; in Botanic Gardens on Stranmillis Road, south of downtown, tel. 028/9044-0000, www.nmni.com.

Visiting the Museum: The five-floor museum is pretty painless. Ride the elevator to the top floor and follow the spiraling exhibits downhill through various zones. The top two floors are dedicated to rotating art exhibits, the next floor down covers local nature, and the two below that focus on history. The ground floor covers the Troubles, and has a coffee shop and gift shop.

The Art Zone displays beautifully crafted fine crystal and china. In the Nature Zone, audiovisuals trace how the Ice Age affected the local landscape. Dinosaur skeletons lurk, stuffed wildlife plays possum, and geology rocks. Kids will enjoy the interactive Discover History room.

The delicately worded History Zone has an interesting British slant (such as the implication that most deaths in the Great Potato Famine of 1845-1849 were caused by typhus and fever epidemics—with little mention of the starvation that made peasants susceptible to these diseases in the first place). But the coverage of the modern-day Troubles is balanced and thought-provoking.

After a peek at a pretty good mummy, top things off with the *Girona* treasure. Soggy bits of gold, silver, leather, and wood were salvaged from the Spanish Armada's shipwrecked *Girona*, lost off the Antrim Coast north of Belfast in 1588.

▲Botanic Gardens

This is the backyard of Queen's University, and on a sunny day, you couldn't imagine a more relaxing park setting. On a cold day, step into the Tropical Ravine for a jungle of heat and humidity. Take a quick walk through the Palm House, reminiscent of the one in London's Kew Gardens, but smaller. The Ulster Museum is on the garden's grounds.

Cost and Hours: Free, gardens open daily 8:00 until dusk; Palm House open daily 10:00-17:00, Oct-March until 16:00; tel. 028/9031-4762, www.belfastcity.gov.uk/parks.

Nearby: Just south of the gardens is the **Lyric Theatre**, an architecturally innovative building rebuilt in 2011 (no tours, but there are performances; see "Entertainment in Belfast," later).

NEAR BELFAST

▲▲Ulster Folk Park and Transport Museum

This sprawling 180-acre, two-museum complex straddles the road and rail line at Cultra, midway between Bangor and Belfast (8 miles east of town).

Cost and Hours: £9 for each museum, £11 combo-ticket for both, £29 for families; March-Sept Tue-Sun 10:00-17:00; Oct-Feb Tue-Fri 10:00-16:00, Sat-Sun 11:00-16:00; closed Mon year-round; check the schedule for the day's special events, tel. 028/9042-8428, www.nmni.com.

Getting There: From Belfast, you can reach Cultra by taxi (£15), bus #502 (2/hour, 30 minutes, from Laganside Bus Centre), or train (2/hour, 15 minutes, from any Belfast train station or from Bangor). Buses stop right in the park, but schedules are skimpy on Saturday and Sunday. Train service is more dependable (and more frequent on the weekend): Get off at the Cultra stop, which puts off between the two parks, a bit closer to the Transport Museum than to the Folk Park.

Planning Your Time: Allow three hours for your visit, and expect lots of walking. Most people will spend an hour in the Transport Museum and a couple of hours at the Folk Park. You'll arrive (by rail or car) between the two museums a bit closer to the Transport Museum. From here, you have a choice of going downhill to the Transport Museum or 200 panting yards uphill into the Folk Park. Assess your energy level and plan accordingly. Those with a car can drive between the museum and the folk park. Note that the Transport Museum is all indoors. The Folk Park involves more walking between buildings spread across the upper hillside.

Visiting the Museums: The **Transport Museum** consists of three buildings. Start at the bottom and trace the evolution of transportation from 7,500 years ago—when people first decided to load an ox—to the first vertical takeoff jet. In 1909, the Belfast-

The Red Hand of Ulster

All over Belfast, you'll notice a curious symbol: a red hand facing you as if swearing a pledge or telling you to halt. You'll spot it, faded, above the Linen Hall Library door, in the wrought-iron fences of the Merchant Hotel, on old-fashioned clothes wringers (in the Ulster Folk Park and Transport Museum at Cultra), above the front door of a bank in Bangor, in the shape of a flowerbed at Mount Stewart House, in Loyalist paramilitary murals, on shield emblems in the gates of Republican memorials, and even on the flag of Northern Ireland (the white flag with the red cross of St. George). It's known as the Red Hand of Ulster—and it is one  of the few emblems used by both communities in Northern Ireland.

Nationalists display a red-hand-on-a-yellow-shield as a symbol of the ancient province of Ulster. It was the official crest of the once-dominant O'Neill clan (who fought tooth and nail against English rule) and today signifies resistance to British rule in these communities.

But you'll more often see the red hand in Unionist areas. They see it as a potent symbol of the political entity of Northern Ireland. The Ulster Volunteer Force chose it for their symbol in 1913 and embedded it in the center of the Northern Irish flag upon partition of the island in 1921. You may see the red hand clenched as a fist in Loyalist murals. One Loyalist paramilitary group even named itself the Red Hand Commandos.

The origin of the red hand comes from a mythological tale of two rival clans that raced by boat to claim a far shore. The first clan leader to touch the shore would win it for his people. Everyone aboard both vessels strained mightily at their oars, near exhaustion as they approached the shore. Finally, in desperation, the chieftain leader of the slower boat whipped out his sword and lopped off his right hand...which he then flung onto the shore, thus winning the coveted land. Moral of the story? The fearless folk of Ulster will do *whatever it takes* to get the job done.

based Shorts Aviation Company partnered with the Wright brothers to manufacture the first commercially available aircraft. The middle building holds an intriguing section on the sinking of the Belfast-made *Titanic*. The top building covers the history of bikes, cars, and trains. The car section rumbles from the first car in Ireland (an 1898 Benz), through the "Cortina Culture" of the 1960s, to the local adventures of controversial automobile designer John DeLorean and a 1981 model of his sleek sports car.

The **Folk Park,** an open-air collection of 34 reconstructed buildings from all over the nine counties of Ulster, showcases the region's traditional lifestyles. After wandering through the old-town site (church, print shop, schoolhouse, humble Belfast row house, silent movie theater, and so on), you'll head off into the country to nip into cottages, farmhouses, and mills. Some houses are warmed by a wonderful peat fire and a friendly attendant. Your visit can be dull or vibrant, depending upon whether attendants are available to chat. Drop a peat brick on the fire.

▲Carrickfergus Castle

Built during the Norman invasion of the late 1100s, this historic castle stands sentry on the shore of Belfast Lough. William of

Orange landed here in 1690, when he began his Irish campaign against deposed King James II. In 1778, the American privateer ship *Ranger* (the first ever to fly the Stars-and-Stripes), under the command of John Paul Jones, defeated the HMS *Drake* just up the coast. These days the castle feels a bit sanitized and geared for kids, but it's an easy excursion if you're seeking a castle experience near the city.

Cost and Hours: £5; daily 10:00-17:00, Oct-March until 16:00; tel. 028/9335-1273.

Getting There: It's a 20-minute train ride from Belfast (on the line to Larne). Turn left as you exit the train station and walk straight downhill for five minutes—all the way to the waterfront—passing under the arch of the old town wall en route. You'll find the castle on your right.

▲The Gobbins Cliff Path

Newly reopened in 2016, the Gobbins Cliff Path is an Edwardian adventure with birds, beautiful scenery, and occasional rogue waves. Located 20 miles northeast of Belfast via Carrickfergus, this complex path—a mix of tunnel bridges, railings, and steps carved, hammered, or fastened to the cliff—was first opened in 1902, designed to boost tourism. Once popular, it fell into disrepair during World War II and was closed for decades. The newly reinforced path (which, to spoil all the turn-of-the-century fun, now requires helmets and guides) takes two to three hours to hike, and is awkward and steep in places, but not terribly strenuous. You'll spot puffins, cormorants, and kittiwakes in nesting areas along the way.

Cost and Hours: £10, visitor center open daily 9:30-17:30, required guided hikes generally hourly (weather permitting), book in advance as tours can fill up, tel. 028/9337-2318, 68 Middle Road, Islandmagee, www.thegobbinscliffpath.com.

Getting There: By car, take the A-2 from Belfast to Larne, turn right on B-90, and follow the signs to *Islandmagee* and *The Gobbins*. Without a car, take a train to Ballycarry (on the Larne line) and walk a mile to the center, or take a taxi (Ballycarry Cabs, tel. 028/9303-8131).

Entertainment in Belfast

Consider the following, as well as the musical pub crawl offered by Belfast Trad Trail Tours (described earlier, under "Tours in Belfast").

Theater
Located beside the River Lagan (near Queen's University), the **Lyric Theatre** is a Belfast institution. Rebuilt in 2011, it represents the cultural rejuvenation of the city—the building was partially funded by donations from actors such as Liam Neeson, Kenneth Branagh, and Meryl Streep. While there are no public tours, it's a good place to see quality local productions (tickets £15-25; box office open daily 10:00-17:00; 55 Ridgeway Street, tel. 028/9038-1081, www.lyrictheatre.co.uk).

Traditional Music and Dance
Belfast Story features former *Riverdance* musicians and dancers for an energetic hour celebrating the people, poetry, and music of Belfast. It's set in a characteristic pub—with the local crowd on the ground floor and the tourists packed into a tiny performance room upstairs (£25; May-Oct Wed and Fri-Sat at 20:00, upstairs in Madden's Pub at 74 Berry Street, tel. 079-7189-5746, www.belfasthiddentours.com).

Sleeping in Belfast

Belfast is more of a business town than a tourist town, so business-class room rates are lower or soft on weekends. For cozy B&Bs, check out the Queen's University area or the nearby seaside town of Bangor.

IN CENTRAL BELFAST

To locate these hotels, see the map on page 72.

$$$$ Hotel Europa is Belfast's landmark hotel—fancy, comfortable, and central—with four stars and lower weekend rates. Modern yet elegant, this place is the choice of visiting diplomats (breakfast extra, Great Victoria Street, tel. 028/9027-1066, www. hastingshotels.com, res@eur.hastingshotels.com).

$$$ Jurys Inn, an American-style hotel that rents 190 identical modern rooms, is perfectly located two blocks from City Hall (breakfast extra, Fisherwick Place, tel. 028/9053-3500, www. jurysinns.com, jurysinnbelfast@jurysinns.com).

SOUTH OF QUEEN'S UNIVERSITY

Many of Belfast's best budget beds cluster in a comfortable, leafy neighborhood just south of Queen's University (near the Ulster Museum). The Botanic, Adelaide, and City Hospital train stations are nearby (I find Botanic the most convenient), and buses zip down Malone Road every 20 minutes. Any bus on Malone Road goes to Donegall Square East. Taxis take you downtown for about £6 (your host can call one).

$$$ Malone Lodge Hotel, by far the classiest listing in this neighborhood, provides slick, business-class comfort in 119 spacious rooms on a quiet street (elevator, restaurant, parking, 60 Eglantine Avenue, tel. 028/9038-8000, www.malonelodgehotel.com, info@malonelodgehotel.com).

$$ Gregory Guesthouse, with its stately red brick, ages gracefully behind a green lawn with 15 large, fresh rooms. It's a good value with subtle charm on a quiet street (family room, parking, 32 Eglantine Ave, tel. 028/9066-3454, www.thegregorybelfast.com, info@thegregorybelfast.com).

$$ Wellington Park Hotel is a dependable, if unimaginative, chain-style hotel with 75 rooms. It's predictable but in a good location (parking extra, 21 Malone Road, tel. 028/9038-1111, www. wellingtonparkhotel.com, info@wellingtonparkhotel.com).

$ Elms Village, a huge Queen's University dorm complex, rents 100 basic, institutional rooms (all singles) to travelers during summer break (July and Aug only, coin-op laundry, self-serve kitchen; reception building is 50 yards down entry street, marked *Elms Village* on low brick wall, 78 Malone Road; tel. 028/9097-4525, www.stayatqueens.com, accommodation@qub.ac.uk).

BETWEEN QUEEN'S UNIVERSITY AND SHAFTESBURY SQUARE

$$ Benedicts Hotel has 32 rooms in a good location at the northern fringe of the Queen's University district. Its popular bar is a maze of polished wood and can be loud on weekend nights (eleva-

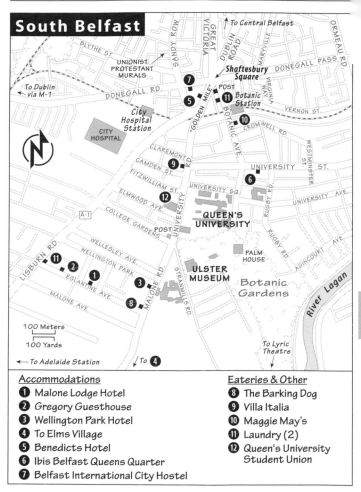

South Belfast

To Central Belfast

Shaftesbury Square

To Dublin via M-1

City Hospital Station

CITY HOSPITAL

QUEEN'S UNIVERSITY

ULSTER MUSEUM

PALM HOUSE

Botanic Gardens

River Lagan

100 Meters
100 Yards

← To Adelaide Station

To Lyric Theatre

BELFAST

Accommodations
1. Malone Lodge Hotel
2. Gregory Guesthouse
3. Wellington Park Hotel
4. To Elms Village
5. Benedicts Hotel
6. Ibis Belfast Queens Quarter
7. Belfast International City Hostel

Eateries & Other
8. The Barking Dog
9. Villa Italia
10. Maggie May's
11. Laundry (2)
12. Queen's University Student Union

tor, 7 Bradbury Place, tel. 028/9059-1999, www.benedictshotel. co.uk, info@benedictshotel.co.uk).

$$ Ibis Belfast Queens Quarter, part of a major European hotel chain, has 56 practical rooms in a convenient location. It's a great deal if you're not looking for cozy character (breakfast extra, elevator, a block north of Queen's University at 75 University Street, tel. 028/9033-3366, www.ibisbelfast.com, h7288-fo@accor.com).

¢ Belfast International City Hostel, big and creatively run, provides the best value among Belfast's hostels. It is located near Botanic Station, in the heart of the lively university district, and has 24-hour reception. Paul, the manager, is a veritable TI, with a passion for his work (private rooms available, 22 Donegall Road, tel. 028/9031-5435, www.hini.org.uk, info@hini.org.uk).

Eating in Belfast

DOWNTOWN

For locations, see the map on page 72 .

The Morning Star is woody and elegant, with a **$$$ restaurant** upstairs (daily 12:00-22:00) and a **$ afternoon buffet** (Mon-Sat 12:00-16:00; down alley just off High Street at 17 Pottinger's Entry, alley entry is roughly opposite the post office, tel. 028/9023-5986).

$$ Robinson & Cleaver has a great central location, perfect for light lunches or tasty dinners. In good weather, their balcony has terrific views of City Hall (Mon-Sat 12:00-15:00, Wed-Sat also 17:00-21:30, closed Sun; Donegall Square North, a few doors east of the TI, tel. 028/9031-2666).

$$$ Coco Restaurant is a spacious, high-end place with a quirky sense of style serving reliably tasty modern Irish and Continental dishes. Their early-bird special makes it a budget find if you order before 19:00 (open nightly from 17:30, a couple of blocks behind City Hall at 7 Linen Hall Street, tel. 028/9031-1150).

$$ Crown Liquor Saloon, a recommended stop along the Golden Mile, is small and antique. Its mesmerizing mishmash of mosaics and shareable snugs (booths—best to reserve) is topped with a smoky tin ceiling (food served Sun-Thu 11:30-19:00, Fri-Sat until 17:00, 46 Great Victoria Street, across from Hotel Europa, tel. 028/9024-3187, www.nicholsonspubs.co.uk). The **$$$ Crown Dining Room** upstairs offers dependable meals (daily 11:30-20:00,

tel. 028/9024-3187, use entry on Amelia Street when the Crown Liquor Saloon is closed).

$$$ Europa Piano Lounge rests serenely above the lobby of the Europa Hotel, with refined service and possibly the best club sandwich in town. It's a great hideaway for quietly recharging your sightseeing batteries (daily 10:00-22:00, tel. 028/9027-1066).

$$ Kelly's Cellars, once a rebel hangout (see plaque above door), still has a very gritty Irish feel. It's 300 years old and hard to find, but worth it. The pub grub is basic, but the atmosphere is delicious (Mon-Sat 11:30-24:30, Sun 13:00-23:30; live traditional music Tue-Fri and Sun at 21:30, Sat at 16:30; 32 Bank Street, 100 yards behind Tesco supermarket, access via alley on left side when facing Tesco, tel. 028/9024-6058).

Lunch Spots: The **$ Bobbin Café** at City Hall is a good, cheap, and cheery little cafeteria serving soups, sandwiches, and hot dishes (open daily, same hours as City Hall). Across the street, the **$ Linen Hall Library Café** is more elegant (it's like eating with professors in a library) but with a more limited lunch menu (daily 9:30-16:00).

Supermarkets: Consider a picnic on the City Hall lawn with food from one of the following. **Marks & Spencer** has a coffee shop and a supermarket in its basement (daily until 18:00, WCs on second floor, Donegall Place, a block north of Donegall Square). **Tesco** is a block north of Marks & Spencer and two blocks north of Donegall Square (open slightly later than Marks & Spencer, Royal Avenue and Bank Street).

CATHEDRAL QUARTER

For restaurant locations, see the map on page 72.

Check out the lobby of **$$$$ Merchant Hotel** (a grand former bank) for a glimpse of crushed-velvet Victorian splendor under an opulent dome, and consider indulging in Belfast's best afternoon tea splurge. Don't show up in shorts and sneakers (£25 for Mon-Fri 12:00-16:30, £29.50 for Sat-Sun, reserve ahead for seating at 12:30 or 15:00, 35 Waring Street, tel. 028/9023-4888, www. themerchanthotel.com).

$$$ 2 Taps Wine Bar is a whiff of Mediterranean warmth in this cold brick city. Try a cheerful tapas or paella meal washed down with sangria (Tue-Sun 12:00-21:00, closed Mon, 42 Waring Street, tel. 028/9031-1414).

$$ The Cloth Ear is a friendly, modern, often-crowded bar serving better-than-average pub grub from the kitchen of the posh Merchant Hotel next door (daily 12:00-20:30, 33 Waring Street, tel. 028/9026-2719).

$$ The Dirty Onion and **Yardbird** are a hip combo filling a dimly lit and woody warehouse with enthusiastic young-at-heart locals. The Yardbird (upstairs) serves the grub, specializing in rotisserie chicken that's "clucking good." The Dirty Onion (downstairs) is a popular pub that spills suds and live music into its packed outer courtyard on summer nights (daily 12:00-23:30, 3 Hill Street, tel. 028/9024-3712).

VICTORIA SQUARE AREA

Although Victoria Square is a big, glitzy mall, a couple of fun options are worth considering—one inside the mall (for food) and one next door (for drinks).

$$ Wagamama, part of a British chain, is a Japanese noodle bar located on the first floor of the mall. Hearty portions of chicken ramen, *yakisoba,* and cumin beef salad are menu highlights (Sun-Wed 12:00-21:00, Thu-Sat until 22:00, Victoria Square, tel. 028/9023-6098).

Bittles Bar is a good place to stop for a pint. It's a tiny, wedge-shaped throwback to Victorian days, hidden in the shadows on the east side of the mall next to the ornate, yellow Victorian fountain. The minuscule, terraced interior is decorated with caricatures of literary and political figures (daily generally 12:00 until late, no food, 70 Upper Church Lane just off Victoria Street, mobile 077-9396-2329).

NEAR QUEEN'S UNIVERSITY
For locations, see the map on page 81.

$$$ The Barking Dog is closest to my cluster of accommodations south of the university. It's a trendy grill serving tasty burgers, duck, scallops, and other filling fare. If the weather's fine, the outdoor tree-shaded front tables are ideal for people-watching (Mon-Sat 12:00-15:00 & 17:00-22:00, Sun 12:00-21:00, near corner of Eglantine Avenue at 33 Malone Road, tel. 028/9066-1885).

$$$ Villa Italia packs in crowds hungry for linguini and *bistecca*. With its checkered tablecloths and a wood-beamed ceiling draped with grape leaves, it's a little bit of Italy in Belfast (Mon-Sat 17:00-23:00, Sun 12:30-21:30, 3 long blocks south of Shaftesbury Square, at intersection with University Street, 39 University Road, tel. 028/9032-8356).

$$ Maggie May's serves hearty, simple, affordable meals (Sun-Thu 8:00-22:00, Fri-Sat until 23:00, one block south of Botanic Station at 50 Botanic Avenue, tel. 028/9032-2662).

Belfast Connections

BY TRAIN OR BUS
For updated schedules and prices for both trains and buses in Northern Ireland, check with Translink (tel. 028/9066-6630, www.translink.co.uk). Consider a Belfast Visitor Pass if you're visiting just Belfast. Those going beyond Belfast can make use of the Zone 4 iLink smartcard, good for all-day train and bus use in Northern Ireland. Service is less frequent on Sundays.

From Belfast by Train to: Dublin (8/day, 2 hours), **Derry** (10/day, 2.5 hours), **Larne** (hourly, 1 hour), **Portrush** (15/day, 2 hours, transfer in Coleraine), **Bangor** (2/hour, 30 minutes). Expect less-frequent service on Sundays.

By Bus to: Portrush (12/day, 2 hours; scenic-coast route, 2.5 hours), **Derry** (hourly, 2 hours), **Dublin** (hourly, most via Dublin Airport, 3 hours), **Galway** (every 2 hours, 6 hours, change in Dublin), **Glasgow** (3/day, 6 hours), **Edinburgh** (3/day, 7 hours). The Europa Bus Centre is behind Hotel Europa (Ulsterbus tel. 028/9033-7003 for destinations in Scotland and England).

BELFAST

BY PLANE

Belfast has two airports. **George Best Belfast City Airport** (airport code: BHD, tel. 028/9093-9093, www.belfastcityairport.com) is a five-minute taxi ride from town (near the docks) or a £2.50 ride on the Airport Express bus #600 (hourly from Europa Bus Centre). Meanwhile, **Belfast International Airport** (airport code: BFS, tel. 028/9448-4848, www.belfastairport.com) is 18 miles west of town—a £7.50 ride on the Airport Express bus #300 (hourly from Europa Bus Centre).

If you're headed for Edinburgh or Glasgow, flying is generally better than taking the ferry (slow and not that scenic), as it's a fairly cheap, short trip.

BY FERRY

To Scotland: You can sail between Belfast and **Cairnryan** on the Stena Line ferry. A Rail Link coach connects the Cairnryan port to Ayr, where you'll catch a train to Glasgow Central station (7/day, 2.5 hours by ferry plus 2.5 hours by bus and train, tel. 028/9074-7747, www.stenaline.co.uk). The P&O Ferry (toll tel. 087-1664-2121, www.poferries.com) goes from **Larne,** 20 miles north of Belfast, to **Cairnryan** (7/day, 2 hours), with bus or rail connections from there to Glasgow and Edinburgh. There are hourly trains between Belfast and Larne (1-hour trip, Larne TI tel. 028/2826-2495).

To England: You can sail from Belfast to **Liverpool** (generally 2/day, 8 hours, arrives in port of Birkenhead—10 minutes from Liverpool, tel. 028/9074-7747, www.stenaline.co.uk).

Bangor

To stay in a laid-back seaside hometown—with more comfort per pound—sleep 12 miles east of Belfast in Bangor (BANG gir). With elegant old homes facing its spruced-up harbor and not even a hint of big-city Belfast, the city has appeal, and it's a handy alternative for travelers who find Belfast booked up by occasional conventions and conferences.

Formerly a Victorian resort and seaside escape from the big city nearby, Bangor now has a sleepy residential feeling. To visit two worthwhile sights near Bangor—the Somme Heritage Centre and Mount Stewart House—consider renting a car for the day (bus service to these sights is sporadic) at nearby George Best Belfast City Airport, a 15-minute train trip from Bangor. The harbor is a 10-minute walk from the train station.

GETTING THERE

Catch the train to Bangor from either Belfast's Central or Great Victoria Street stations; both are on the same line and cost the same (2/hour, 30 minutes, go to the end of the line—don't get off at Bangor West). Consider stopping en route at Cultra (Ulster Folk Park and Transport Museum). The journey gives you a good, close-up look at the giant Belfast harbor cranes.

If day-tripping into Belfast from Bangor, get off at Central Station (free shuttle bus to town center, 4/hour, none on Sun; some trains may also stop at the more convenient Great Victoria Street Station), or stay on until Botanic Station for the Ulster Museum, the Golden Mile, and Sandy Row. Trains cost the same from Bangor to all three Belfast stations (Central Station, Great Victoria Station, and Botanic Station).

Orientation to Bangor

Tourist Information: Bangor's TI is in a stone tower house (from 1637) on the harborfront (Mon-Fri 9:15-17:00, Sat from 10:00, Sun 13:00-17:00 except closed Sun Sept-April, 34 Quay Street, tel. 028/9127-0069, www.visitardsandnorthdown.com).

Helpful Hints: You'll find **Speediwash Launderette** at 96 Abbey Street, a couple of blocks south of the train station (Mon-Sat 9:00-18:00, closed Sun, tel. 028/9127-0074). **Kare Cabs** provides local taxi service (tel. 028/9145-6777 or 028/9181-8001).

Sights in Bangor

Walks

For sightseeing, your time is better spent in Belfast. But if you have time to burn in Bangor, enjoy a walk next to the water on the **Coastal Path,** which leads west out of town from the marina. A pleasant three-mile walk along the water leads you to Crawfordsburn Country Park in the suburb of Helen's Bay. Hidden in the trees above Helen's Bay beach is Grey Point Fort, with its two WWI artillery bunkers guarding the shore (generally Sat-Sun 12:00-16:00, tel. 028/9185-3621). Allow 1.5 hours each way as you share the easy-to-follow and mostly paved trail with local joggers, dog walkers, and bikers.

For a shorter walk with views of the marina, head to the end of the **North Pier,** where you'll find a mosaic honoring the D-Day

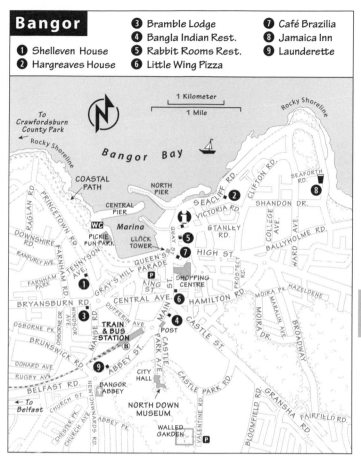

Bangor

❶ Shelleven House
❷ Hargreaves House
❸ Bramble Lodge
❹ Bangla Indian Rest.
❺ Rabbit Rooms Rest.
❻ Little Wing Pizza
❼ Café Brazilia
❽ Jamaica Inn
❾ Launderette

fleet that rendezvoused offshore in 1944, far from Nazi reconnaissance aircraft. Keep an eye out in the marina for Rose the seal. Little kids may enjoy the **Pickie Fun Park** next to the marina, with paddleboat swan rides and miniature golf. The **Bangor Castle** grounds are good for picnics, and include a peaceful walled garden (free, open Mon-Thu 10:00-17:00, Fri-Sun until 18:00).

North Down Museum

This museum covers local history, from monastic days to Viking raids to Victorian splendor. It's hidden on the grassy grounds behind the City Hall, uphill and opposite from the train station.

Cost and Hours: Free, July-Aug daily 10:00-16:30; Sept-June Tue-Sat 10:00-16:30, Sun from 12:00, closed Mon, tel. 028/9127-1200.

NEAR BANGOR

The eastern fringe of Northern Ireland is populated mostly by people who consider themselves true-blue British citizens with a history of loyalty to the Crown that goes back more than 400 years. Two sights within reach by car from Bangor highlight this area's firm roots in British culture: the Somme Heritage Centre and Mount Stewart House. Call ahead to confirm sight opening hours.

Getting There: Bus service from Bangor is patchy (bus #6; check schedule with Bangor TI). I'd rent a car instead at nearby George Best Belfast City Airport, which is only 15 minutes by train from Bangor or 10 minutes from Belfast's Central Station. Because the airport is east of Belfast, your drive to these rural sights skips the headache of urban Belfast.

▲Mount Stewart House

No manor house in Ireland better illuminates the affluent lifestyle of the Protestant ascendancy than this lush estate. After the defeat of James II (the last Catholic king of England) at the Battle of the Boyne in 1690, the Protestant monarchy was in control—and the privileged status of landowners of the same faith was assured. In the 1700s, Ireland's many Catholic rebellions seemed finally to be squashed, so Anglican landlords felt

safe flaunting their wealth in manor houses surrounded by utterly perfect gardens. The Mount Stewart House in particular was designed to dazzle.

Cost and Hours: £9.50 for house and gardens; daily 10:00-16:30, closed Nov-Feb; 8 miles south of Bangor, just off A-20 beside Strangford Lough, tel. 028/4278-8387, www.nationaltrust.org.uk, enquiries@nationaltrust.org.uk.

Visiting the House: Hourly tours give you a glimpse of the cushy life led by the Marquess of Londonderry and his heirs over

the past three centuries. The main entry hall is a stunner, with a black-and-white checkerboard tile floor, marble columns, classical statues, and pink walls supporting a balcony with a domed ceiling and a fine chandelier. In the dining room, you'll see the original seats occupied by the rears of European heads of state, brought back from the Congress of Vienna after Napoleon's 1815 defeat. A huge

BELFAST

painting of Hambletonian, a prize-winning racehorse, hangs above the grand staircase, dwarfing a portrait of the Duke of Wellington in a hall nearby. The heroic duke (worried that his Irish birth would be seen as lower class by British blue bloods) once quipped in Parliament, "Just because one is born in a stable does not make him a horse." Irish emancipator Daniel O'Connell retorted, "Yes, but it could make you an ass."

Afterward, wander the expansive manicured **gardens.** The fantasy life of parasol-toting, upper-crust Victorian society seems to ooze from every viewpoint. Fanciful sculptures of extinct dodo birds and monkeys holding vases on their heads set off predictably classic Italian and Spanish sections. An Irish harp has been trimmed out of a hedge a few feet from a flowerbed shaped like the Red Hand of Ulster. Swans glide serenely among the lily pads on a small lake.

Somme Heritage Centre

World War I's trench warfare was a meat grinder. More British soldiers died in the last year of that war than in all of World War II. Northern Ireland's men were not spared—especially during the bloody Battle of the Somme in France, starting in July 1916. Among the Allied forces was the British Army's 36th Ulster Division, which drew heavily from this loyal heartland of Northern Ireland. The 36th Ulster Division suffered brutal losses at the Battle of the Somme—of the 760 men recruited from the Shankill Road area in Belfast, only 10 percent survived.

Exhibits portray the battle experience through a mix of military artifacts, photos, historical newsreels, and life-size figures posed in trench warfare re-creations. To access the majority of the exhibits, it's essential to take the one-hour guided tour (leaving hourly, on the hour). Visiting this place is a moving experience, but it can only hint at the horrific conditions endured by these soldiers.

Cost and Hours: £6.50; July-Aug Mon-Fri 10:00-16:00, Sat from 11:00, closed Fri Sept-June and Sun year-round; hourly tours, 3 miles south of Bangor just off A-21 at 233 Bangor Road, tel. 028/9182-3202, www.irishsoldier.org. A coffee shop is located at the center.

Sleeping in Bangor

Visitors arriving in Bangor (by train) come down Main Street to reach the harbor marina. You'll find Hargreaves House to the right, along the waterfront east of the marina on Seacliff Road. The other two listings are to the left, just uphill and west of the marina.

$$$ Shelleven House is an old-fashioned, well-kept, stately place with 13 prim rooms on the quiet corner of Princetown Road and Tennyson Avenue (RS%, parking, 61 Princetown Road, tel. 028/9127-1777, www.shellevenhouse.com, info@shellevenhouse. com, Sue and Paul Toner).

$$ Hargreaves House, a homey Victorian waterfront refuge with three cozy rooms, is Bangor's best value (RS%—use code HHRS18, 15-minute walk from train station but worth it, 78 Seacliff Road, tel. 028/9146-4071, mobile 079-8058-5047, www. hargreaveshouse.com, info@hargreaveshouse.com, Pauline Mendez).

$$ Bramble Lodge is closest to the train station (10-minute walk), offering three inviting and spotless rooms (1 Bryansburn Road, tel. 028/9145-7924, mobile 077-9262-8001, jacquihanna_bramblelodge@yahoo.co.uk, Jacquiline Hanna).

Eating in Bangor

Be aware that most restaurants in town stop seating at about 20:30.

$$$ Bangla serves fine Indian cuisine with attentive service and a good-value early-bird option before 19:00 (daily 12:00-14:30, also Thu-Sun 16:30-23:00, 115 Main Street, tel. 028/9127-1272).

The **$$ Rabbit Rooms** serves hearty Irish food to local crowds (daily 12:00-21:00, near the harbor at 33 Quay Street, tel. 028/9146-7699).

$ Little Wing Pizza is a friendly joint serving tasty pizza, pasta, and salads. Grab your food to go and munch by the marina. It's also one of the few places in town that serves food later at night (daily 11:00-22:00, 37 Main Street, tel. 028/9147-2777).

$ Café Brazilia, a popular locals' lunch hangout with a simple menu, is across from the stubby clock tower (Mon-Sat 8:00-16:30, Sun from 10:00, 13 Bridge Street, tel. 028/9127-2763).

The **$$ Jamaica Inn** offers pleasant pub grub and a breezy waterfront porch (food served about 12:00-21:00, 10-minute walk east of the TI, 188 Seacliff Road, tel. 028/9147-1610).

BELFAST

PRACTICALITIES

This section covers just the basics on traveling in Northern Ireland (for much more information, see *Rick Steves Ireland*). You'll find free advice on specific topics at www.ricksteves.com/tips.

While it shares an island with the Republic of Ireland, Northern Ireland is part of the United Kingdom—which makes its currency, phone codes, and other practicalities different from the Republic.

Money

For currency, Northern Ireland uses the pound (£): 1 pound (£1) = about $1.30. One pound is broken into 100 pence (p). To convert prices in pounds to dollars, add about 30 percent: £20 = about $25, £50 = about $65. (Check www.oanda.com for the latest exchange rates.) While the pound used here is called the "Ulster Pound," it's interchangeable with the British pound.

The standard way for travelers to get local currency is to withdraw money from an ATM (which locals may call a "cash point") using a debit card, ideally with a Visa or MasterCard logo. To keep your cash, cards, and valuables safe, wear a money belt.

Before departing, call your bank or credit-card company: Confirm that your card(s) will work overseas, ask about international transaction fees, and alert them that you'll be making withdrawals in Europe. Also ask for the PIN number for your credit card—you may need it for Europe's "chip-and-PIN" payment machines (see below; allow time for your bank to mail your PIN to you).

Dealing with "Chip and PIN": Most credit and debit cards now have chips that authenticate and secure transactions.

European cardholders insert their chip card into the payment slot, then enter a PIN. (For most US cards, you provide a signature.) Any American card, whether with a chip or an old-fashioned magnetic stripe, will work at Europe's hotels, restaurants, and shops. But some self-service chip-and-PIN payment machines—such as those at train stations, toll roads, or unattended gas pumps—may not accept your card, even if you know the PIN. If your card won't work, look for a cashier who can process the transaction manually—or pay in cash.

Dynamic Currency Conversion: If merchants or hoteliers offer to convert your purchase price into dollars (called dynamic currency conversion, or DCC), refuse this "service." You'll pay extra in fees for the expensive convenience of seeing your charge in dollars. If an ATM offers to "lock in" or "guarantee" your conversion rate, choose "proceed without conversion." Other prompts might state, "You can be charged in dollars: Press YES for dollars, NO for pounds." Always choose the local currency.

Staying Connected

The simplest solution is to bring your own device—mobile phone, tablet, or laptop—and use it just as you would at home (following the tips below, such as connecting to free Wi-Fi whenever possible).

To call Northern Ireland from a US or Canadian number: Whether you're phoning from a landline, your own mobile phone, or a Skype account, you're making an international call. Dial 011-44 and then 28 (Northern Ireland's area code, minus its initial zero), followed by the local number. (The 011 is our international access code, and 44 is the UK's country code.) If dialing from a mobile phone, you can enter + in place of the international access code—press and hold the 0 key.

To call Northern Ireland from a European country: Dial 00-44 followed by 28 and the local number. (The 00 is Europe's international access code.)

To call within Northern Ireland and the UK: All of Northern Ireland shares one area code (028), making all calls within the country local—so you can leave off the area code and simply dial the local number if you're dialing from a local landline. But if you're calling from a mobile phone, or to or from elsewhere in the UK, you need to include the area code.

To call from Northern Ireland to another country: Dial 00 followed by the country code (for example, 1 for the US or Canada), then the area code and number. If you're calling European countries whose phone numbers begin with 0, you'll usually have to omit that 0 when you dial.

Sleep Code

Hotels are classified based on the average price of a typical en suite double room with breakfast in high season.

$$$$	**Splurge:** Most rooms over €140
$$$	**Expensive:** €110-140
$$	**Moderate:** €80-110
$	**Budget:** €50-80
¢	**Backpacker:** Under €50
RS%	**Rick Steves discount**

Unless otherwise noted, credit cards are accepted and free Wi-Fi is available; at B&Bs, you'll likely need to pay cash for your room. Comparison-shop by checking prices at several hotels (on each hotel's own website, on a booking site, or by email). For the best deal, *book directly with the hotel*. If the listing includes **RS%,** request a Rick Steves discount.

Tips: If you bring your own mobile phone, consider getting an international plan; most providers offer a global calling plan that cuts the per-minute cost of phone calls and texts, and a flat-fee data plan.

Use Wi-Fi whenever possible. Most hotels and many cafés offer free Wi-Fi, and you'll likely also find it at tourist information offices, major museums, and public-transit hubs. With Wi-Fi you can use your phone or tablet to make free or inexpensive domestic and international calls via a calling app such as Skype, FaceTime, or Google+ Hangouts. When you can't find Wi-Fi, you can use your cellular network to connect to the Internet, send texts, or make voice calls. When you're done, avoid further charges by manually switching off "data roaming" or "cellular data."

It's possible to stay connected without a mobile device. You can make calls from your hotel (or the increasingly rare public phone), and check email or browse websites using public computers. Most hotels charge a high fee for international calls—ask for rates before you dial.

For more on phoning, see www.ricksteves.com/phoning. For a one-hour talk on "Traveling with a Mobile Device," see www.ricksteves.com/travel-talks.

Sleeping

I've categorized my recommended accommodations based on price, indicated with a dollar-sign rating (see sidebar). I recommend reserving rooms in advance, particularly during peak season. Once your dates are set, check the specific price for your preferred stay at several hotels. You can do this either by comparing prices on Hotels.com or Booking.com, or by checking the hotels' own

Restaurant Price Code

I've assigned each eatery a price category, based on the average cost of a typical main course. Drinks, desserts, and splurge items (steak and seafood) can raise the price considerably.

$$$$	**Splurge:** Most main courses over €25/£20
$$$	**Pricier:** €20-25/£15-20
$$	**Moderate:** €15-20/£10-15
$	**Budget:** Under €15/£10

In Northern Ireland, carryout fish-and-chips and other takeout food is **$**; a basic pub or sit-down eatery is **$$**; a gastropub or casual but more upscale restaurant is **$$$**; and a swanky splurge is **$$$$**.

websites. To get the best deal, contact my family-run hotels directly by phone or email. When you go direct, the owner avoids any third-party commission, giving them wiggle room to offer you a discount, a nicer room, or free breakfast. If you prefer to book online or are considering a hotel chain, it's to your advantage to use the hotel's website.

For complicated requests, send an email with the following information: number and type of rooms; number of nights; arrival date; departure date; and any special requests. Hoteliers typically ask for your credit-card number as a deposit. The prices I list include a hearty breakfast (unless otherwise noted).

Know the terminology: An "en suite" room has a bathroom (toilet and shower/tub) actually inside the room; a room with a "private bathroom" can mean that the bathroom is all yours, but it's across the hall. A "standard" room could have two meanings. Big hotels in the UK sometimes call a basic en-suite room a "standard" room to differentiate it from a fancier "superior" or "deluxe" room. At small hotels and B&Bs, guests in a "standard" room have access to a bathroom that's shared with other rooms and down the hall.

Some hotels are willing to make a deal to attract guests: Try emailing several hotels to ask for their best price. In general, hotel prices can soften if you do any of the following: stay in a "standard" room, offer to pay cash, stay at least three nights, or travel off-season.

Eating

I've categorized my recommended eateries based on price, indicated with a dollar-sign rating (see sidebar). The traditional "Ulster Fry" breakfast includes juice, tea or coffee, cereal, eggs, bacon, sausage, toast, a grilled tomato, sautéed mushrooms, and black pudding. If that's too much for you, order only the items you want.

To dine affordably at classier restaurants, look for "early-bird specials" (offered about 17:30–19:00, last order by 19:00).

Smart travelers use pubs (short for "public houses") to eat, drink, and make new friends. Pub grub is Northern Ireland's best eating value. For about $15–20, you'll get a basic hot lunch or dinner. The menu is hearty and traditional: stews, soups, fish-and-chips, meat, cabbage, potatoes, and—in coastal areas—fresh seafood. Order drinks and meals at the bar. Pay as you order, and don't tip.

Most pubs have lagers (cold, refreshing, American-style beer), ales (amber-colored, cellar-temperature beer), bitters (hop-flavored ale, perhaps the most typical British beer), and stouts (dark and somewhat bitter—the most famous is Guinness, of course).

Tipping: At a sit-down place with table service, tip about 10 percent—unless the service charge is already listed on the bill. If you order at a counter, there's no need to tip.

Transportation

By Car: A car is a worthless headache in Belfast. But if venturing into the countryside, I enjoy the freedom of a rental car for reaching far-flung rural sights. It's cheaper to arrange most car rentals from the US. For route planning, consult www.viamichelin.com, and for tips on your car insurance options, see www.ricksteves.com/cdw (if you're also going to the Republic of Ireland, note that many credit-card companies do not offer collision coverage for rentals in the Republic). Bring your driver's license.

Some companies in Northern Ireland won't rent to anyone over 69. In the Republic of Ireland, you generally can't rent a car if you're 75 or older (unless you have a note from your doctor), and you'll usually pay extra if you're 70-74. In Northern Ireland, the speed limit is in miles per hour; in the Republic, it's in kilometers per hour.

Remember that people throughout Ireland drive on the left side of the road (and the driver sits on the right side of the car). You'll quickly master the many roundabouts: Traffic moves clockwise, cars inside the roundabout have the right-of-way, and entering traffic yields (look to your right as you merge). Note that "camera cops" strictly enforce speed limits by automatically snapping photos of speeders' license plates, then mailing them a bill. Also be aware that your US credit and debit cards with a chip may not work at self-service gas pumps and automated parking garages, but if you know your PIN, try it anyway. The easiest solution is carrying sufficient cash.

Local road etiquette is similar to that in the US. Ask your car-rental company for details, or check the US State Department website (www.travel.state.gov, search for United Kingdom in the

PRACTICALITIES

"Learn about your destination" box, then click on "Travel and Transportation").

By Train and Bus: You can check train and bus schedules at www.translink.co.uk, or call 028/9066-6630. To see if a rail pass could save you money, check www.ricksteves.com/rail. Long-distance buses (called "coaches") are about a third slower than trains, but they're also much cheaper. Bus stations are normally at or near train stations.

Helpful Hints

Emergency Help: To summon the **police** or an **ambulance,** dial 999. For passport problems, call the **US Consulate** (in Belfast, tel. 028/9038-6100, after-hours emergency mobile 012-5350-1106). The **Canadian Consulate** in Belfast (tel. 028/9754-2405) doesn't offer passport services; instead contact the Canadian High Commission in London (tel. 020/7004-6000). For other concerns, get advice from your hotel.

Theft or Loss: To replace a passport, you'll need to go in person to an embassy or consulate (see above). Cancel and replace your credit and debit cards by calling these 24-hour US numbers collect: Visa—tel. 303/967-1096, MasterCard—tel. 636/722-7111, American Express—tel. 336/393-1111. In Northern Ireland and the rest of Britain, to make a collect call to the US, dial 0-800-89-0011; press zero or stay on the line for an operator. File a police report either on the spot or within a day or two; you'll need it to submit an insurance claim for lost or stolen rail passes or travel gear, and it can help with replacing your passport or electronics. For more information, see www.ricksteves.com/help.

Time: Northern Ireland uses the 24-hour clock. It's the same through 12:00 noon, then keep going: 13:00, 14:00, and so on. Ireland, like Great Britain, is five/eight hours ahead of the East/West Coasts of the US (and one hour earlier than most of continental Europe).

Holidays and Festivals: Northern Ireland celebrates many holidays, which can close sights and attract crowds (book hotel rooms ahead). For information on holidays and festivals, check Northern Ireland's tourism website: www.discovernorthernireland.com. For a simple list showing major—though not all—events, see www.ricksteves.com/festivals.

Numbers and Stumblers: What Americans call the second floor of a building is the first floor in Northern Ireland. Local people write dates as day/month/year, so Christmas 2019 is 25/12/19. For most measurements, Northern Ireland uses the metric system: A kilogram is 2.2 pounds, and a liter is about a quart. For driving distances, they use miles.

PRACTICALITIES

Resources from Rick Steves

This Snapshot guide is excerpted from my latest edition of *Rick Steves Ireland,* one of many titles in my ever-expanding series of guidebooks on European travel. I also produce a public television series, *Rick Steves' Europe,* and a public radio show, *Travel with Rick Steves.* My website, www.ricksteves.com, offers free travel information, a forum for travelers' comments, guidebook updates, my travel blog, an online travel store, and information on European rail passes and our tours of Europe. If you're bringing a mobile device, my free Rick Steves Audio Europe app features dozens of self-guided audio tours of the top sights in Europe, and travel interviews about Ireland. You can get Rick Steves Audio Europe via Apple's App Store, Google Play, or the Amazon Appstore. For more information, see www.ricksteves.com/audioeurope.

Additional Resources

Northern Ireland Tourist Information: www.discovernorthernireland.com
Republic of Ireland Tourist Information: www.discoverireland.com
Passports and Red Tape: www.travel.state.gov
Packing List: www.ricksteves.com/packing
Travel Insurance: www.ricksteves.com/insurance
Cheap Flights: www.kayak.com or www.google.com/flights
Airplane Carry-on Restrictions: www.tsa.gov/travelers
Updates for This Book: www.ricksteves.com/update

How Was Your Trip?

To share your tips, concerns, and discoveries after using this book, please fill out the survey at www.ricksteves.com/feedback. Thanks in advance—it helps a lot.

PRACTICALITIES

INDEX

Explore Europe

At ricksteves.com you can browse through thousands of articles, videos, photos and radio interviews, plus find a wealth of money-saving travel tips for planning your dream trip. And with our mobile-friendly website, you can easily access all this great travel information anywhere you go.

TV Shows

Preview the places you'll visit by watching entire half-hour episodes of Rick Steves' Europe (choose from all 100 shows) on-demand, for free.

ricksteves.com

your travel dreams into affordable reality

Radio Interviews

Enjoy ready access to Rick's vast library of radio interviews covering travel

tips and cultural insights that relate specifically to your Europe travel plans.

Travel Forums

Learn, ask, share! Our online community of savvy travelers is a great resource for first-time travelers to Europe, as well as seasoned pros. You'll find forums on each country, plus travel tips and restaurant/hotel reviews. You can even ask one of our well-traveled staff to chime in with an opinion.

Travel News

Subscribe to our free Travel News e-newsletter, and get monthly updates from Rick on what's happening in Europe.

Audio Europe™

Rick's Free Travel App

Get your FREE **Rick Steves Audio Europe**™ app to enjoy...

- Dozens of self-guided tours of Europe's top museums, sights and historic walks

- Hundreds of tracks filled with cultural insights and sightseeing tips from Rick's radio interviews

- All organized into handy geographic playlists

- For Apple and Android

With Rick whispering in your ear, Europe gets even better.

Pack Light and Right

Gear up for your next adventure at ricksteves.com

Light Luggage

Pack light and right with Rick Steves' affordable, custom-designed rolling carry-on bags, backpacks, day packs and shoulder bags.

Accessories

From packing cubes to moneybelts and beyond, Rick has personally selected the travel goodies that will help your trip go smoother.

Rick Steves has

Experience maximum Europe

Save time and energy

This guidebook is your independent-travel toolkit. But for all it delivers, it's still up to you to devote the time and energy it takes to manage the preparation and logistics that are essential for a happy trip. If that's a hassle, there's a solution.

Rick Steves Tours

A Rick Steves tour takes you to Europe's most interesting places with great

great tours, too!

with minimum stress

guides and small groups of 28 or less. We follow Rick's favorite itineraries, ride in comfy buses, stay in family-run hotels, and bring you intimately

close to the Europe you've traveled so far to see. Most importantly, we take away the logistical headaches so you can focus on the fun.

travelers—nearly half of them repeat customers— along with us on four dozen different itineraries, from Ireland to Italy to Athens. Is a Rick Steves tour the

right fit for your travel dreams? Find out at ricksteves.com, where you can also request Rick's latest tour catalog. Europe is best

Join the fun

This year we'll take thousands of free-spirited

experienced with happy travel partners. We hope you can join us.

See our itineraries at ricksteves.com

A Guide for Every Trip

BEST OF GUIDES

Full color easy-to-scan format, focusing on Europe's most popular destinations and sights.

Best of France
Best of Germany
Best of England
Best of Europe
Best of Ireland
Best of Italy
Best of Spain

COMPREHENSIVE GUIDES

City, country, and regional guides with detailed coverage for a multi-week trip exploring the most iconic sights and venturing off the beaten track.

Amsterdam & the Netherlands
Barcelona
Belgium: Bruges, Brussels,
  Antwerp & Ghent
Berlin
Budapest
Croatia & Slovenia
Eastern Europe
England
Florence & Tuscany
France
Germany
Great Britain
Greece: Athens & the Peloponnese
Iceland
Ireland
Istanbul
Italy
London
Paris
Portugal
Prague & the Czech Republic
Provence & the French Riviera
Rome
Scandinavia
Scotland
Spain
Switzerland
Venice
Vienna, Salzburg & Tirol

Rick Steves guidebooks are published by Avalon Travel,
an imprint of Perseus Books, a Hachette Book Group company

OCKET GUIDES

ompact, full color city guides with e essentials for shorter trips.

nsterdam	Paris
:hens	Prague
arcelona	Rome
orence	Venice
ıly's Cinque Terre	Vienna
ondon	
unich & Salzburg	

NAPSHOT GUIDES

ocused single-destination coverage.

asque Country: Spain & France
openhagen & the Best of Denmark
ublin
ubrovnik
dinburgh
ll Towns of Central Italy
rakow, Warsaw & Gdansk
sbon
oire Valley
adrid & Toledo
ılan & the Italian Lakes District
aples & the Amalfi Coast
orthern Ireland
ormandy
orway
eykjavik
evilla, Granada & Southern Spain
.. Petersburg, Helsinki & Tallinn
.ockholm

CRUISE PORTS GUIDES

Reference for cruise ports of call.

Mediterranean Cruise Ports
Northern European Cruise Ports

Complete your library with...

TRAVEL SKILLS & CULTURE

Study up on travel skills and gain insight on history and culture.

Europe 101
European Christmas
European Easter
European Festivals
Europe Through the Back Door
Postcards from Europe
Travel as a Political Act

PHRASE BOOKS & DICTIONARIES

French
French, Italian & German
German
Italian
Portuguese
Spanish

PLANNING MAPS

Britain, Ireland & London
Europe
France & Paris
Germany, Austria & Switzerland
Ireland
Italy
Spain & Portugal

Avalon Travel
Hachette Book Group
1700 Fourth Street
Berkeley, CA 94710

For the latest on Rick's lectures, guidebooks, tours, public television series, and public
radio show, contact Rick Steves' Europe, 130 Fourth Avenue North, Edmonds, WA
98020, tel. 425/771-8303, www.ricksteves.com, rick@ricksteves.com.

Rick Steves' Europe
Managing Editor: Jennifer Madison Davis
Special Publications Manager: Risa Laib
Assistant Managing Editor: Cathy Lu
Editors: Glenn Eriksen, Tom Griffin, Katherine Gustafson, Suzanne Kotz, Rosie
Leutzinger, Carrie Shepherd
Editorial & Production Assistant: Jessica Shaw
Editorial Intern: Claire Connor
Contributor: Gene Openshaw
Graphic Content Director: Sandra Hundacker
Maps & Graphics: David C. Hoerlein, Lauren Mills, Mary Rostad

Avalon Travel
Senior Editor and Series Manager: Madhu Prasher
Editor: Jamie Andrade
Associate Editor: Sierra Machado
Copy Editor: Denise Silva
Proofreader: Patrick Collins, Patty Mon
Indexer: Stephen Callahan
Production & Typesetting: Krista Anderson, Lisi Baldwin, Rue Flaherty, Christine
DeLorenzo
Cover Design: Kimberly Glyder Design
Maps & Graphics: Kat Bennett

Photo Credits
Front Cover: Giant's Causeway in North Antrim, Northern Ireland © Aitor Muñoz
Muñoz | Dreamstime
Title Page: Dunluce Castle, County Antrim, Northern Ireland © Richard
Semik/123rf.com
Additional Photography: Dominic Arizona Bonuccelli, Rich Earl, Trish Feaster,
David C. Hoerlein, Pat O'Connor, Rick Steves, Wikimedia Commons (PD-Art/
PD-US). Photos are used by permission and are the property of the original copyright
owners.

ABOUT THE AUTHORS

RICK STEVES

Since 1973, Rick has spent about four months a year exploring Europe. His mission: to empower Americans to have European trips that are fun, affordable, and culturally broadening. Rick produces a best-selling guidebook series, a public television series, and a public radio show, and organizes small-group tours that take over 20,000 travelers to Europe annually. He does all of this with the help of a hardworking, well-traveled staff of 100 at Rick Steves' Europe in Edmonds, Washington, near Seattle. When not on the road, Rick is active in his church and with advocacy groups focused on economic justice, drug policy reform, and ending hunger. To recharge, Rick plays piano, relaxes at his family cabin in the Cascade Mountains, and spends time with his partner Trish, son Andy, and daughter Jackie. Find out more about Rick at www.ricksteves.com and on Facebook.

PAT O'CONNOR

Pat O'Connor, an Irish-American, first journeyed to Ireland in 1981 and was hooked by the history and passion of the feisty Irish culture. Frequent return visits led to his partnership with Rick, his work as an Ireland tour guide for Rick Steves' Europe, and co-authorship of this book. Pat, who loves all things Hibernian except the black pudding, thrives on the adventures that occur as he slogs the bogs and drives the Irish back lanes (over 2,000 kilometers annually) in search of new discoveries.

More for your trip!
Maximize the experience with Rick Steves as your guide

Guidebooks
Make side trips smooth and affordable with Rick's England and Scotland guides

Planning Maps
Use Rick's pre-trip planning tool for mapping out your itinerary

Rick's TV Shows
Preview your destinations with a variety of shows covering Ireland

Rick's Audio Europe™ App
Get free travel information for Ireland

Small Group Tours
Take a lively, low-stress Rick Steves tour through Ireland